POOR LATINO
FAMILIES
AND SCHOOL
PREPARATION

ARE THEY DOING THE RIGHT THINGS?

WILLIAM A. SAMPSON

A SCARECROWEDUCATION BOOK

The Scarecrow Press, Inc.
Lanham, Maryland, and Oxford
2003

A SCARECROWEDUCATION BOOK

Published in the United States of America
by Scarecrow Press, Inc.
A Member of the Rowman & Littlefield Publishing Group
4501 Forbes Boulevard, Suite 200, Lanham, Maryland 20706
www.scarecroweducation.com

PO Box 317
Oxford
OX2 9RU, UK

British Library Cataloguing in Publication Information Available

Library of Congress Cataloging-in-Publication Data
Sampson, William A., 1946–
    Poor Latino families and school preparation : are they doing the right
things? / William A. Sampson.
        p. cm.
"A ScarecrowEducation book."
    Includes bibliographical references and index.
    ISBN 0-8108-4682-9 (pbk. : alk. paper)
    1. Hispanic Americans—Education. 2. Poor—Education—United States.
3. Home and school—United States. 4. Academic achievement—United
States. I. Title
LC2670 .S36 2003
371.829'68073—dc21
                                                                    2002153430

∞™ The paper used in this publication meets the minimum requirements of
American National Standard for Information Sciences—Permanence of Paper
for Printed Library Materials, ANSI/NISO Z39.48-1992.
Manufactured in the United States of America.

CONTENTS

PREFACE

In the past dozen years Chicago's public school system has tried to improve the quality of the education offered to poor nonwhite children, who now make up the majority of its students. The city has tried decentralized governance, recentralized governance, charter schools, and more testing. Now it wants to consider longer school days. All of these efforts have two things in common: all are school based, and all will fail. The same can be said for the voucher effort in Milwaukee and Cleveland, the privatization effort in Philadelphia, and the recentralization effort in New York.

All of these attempts to improve the education offered to poor urban nonwhite students revolve around changes in schools. Education policy makers and administrators are well aware that many, if not most, urban schools serving this population are doing a very poor job, and they mistakenly believe that to change this, they should tamper with the things over which they have control. So, they tamper with the length of the school day and the way education is funded. They play around with the length of the school year and the oversight of the schools. They do all these things although there is little empirical evidence that any of these changes will actually significantly improve the education offered to those most in need of a quality education. Then why do they do these things? Simply because they can, and because they do not know what else to do.

School folks can change schools, so they do. The fact that these changes do not seem to solve our problems does not appear to matter too much to them. I do not want to suggest that education policy makers and administrators do not care about the education given to the poor, to nonwhites. Most of them care deeply. They just know only about schools, so that is their focus. But that focus is, in my opinion and on the basis of my data and the data of several others, misplaced.

Many urban schools can be improved. Teaching can be better. Teachers can be more dedicated and motivated. Halls can be cleaner. Students can have more textbooks. If, however, we are really serious about improving education in urban settings, I submit that we need to begin to focus more on changes in families. Students sent to school prepared by their families to learn do much better than those who are not prepared, and schools are not families.

In an effort to study the impact of the family upon the academic success of poor black students in an urban school system, I observed twelve poor black families with middle school students in Evanston, Illinois, for two months and published the results of that work in 2002. Soon after I completed that research, I was approached by one of my Latina students, Denisse Chapa-Malacara, who asked why I had not studied poor Latino families to try to determine the degree to which they were properly preparing their children for the educational experience. The more I thought about this question and considered the rapid growth of the Latino population in a number of our cities, the more intriguing the question became to me.

I decided to "replicate" the first study, this time observing poor Latino families in the same city, Evanston, and in some cases in the same community as the poor black families I had studied. The issue for me was the degree to which these poor Latino families, almost all of whom have parents born in Mexico, prepared their children for school in ways that would maximize their chances of academic success. This work, like the earlier work, is based upon the premise that the best opportunity for the greatest improvement in education comes not in schools but in families. Clearly, a number of poor nonwhite parents do the things necessary to prepare their children to be successful in school. They stress the importance of education, not just in their words, but also in what they do with their children. They focus upon the child's gaining positive self-esteem, internal control, the ability to delay gratification, discipline, the ability to cooperate, responsibility, and a future orientation. They maintain a home environment that is conducive to learning these lessons as well as school lessons.

The question in this volume is, to what degree do poor, urban, Latino families do these things? What is the role of the language difference? What about culture? In this research, unlike the first study with poor blacks in which I focused upon students in their middle school years, I observed every child in each of the eight families. So, I had to pay attention to issues concerning preschool education as well as language and culture.

This work owes a great deal to my own parents, Dorris and William, who stressed for my sisters and me the values, beliefs, and attitudes that we needed to do well in school and that allowed us to climb out of poverty. The work would not have been possible without the efforts of a number of my Latino students at DePaul University who not only urged me on and supported and encouraged me but also did the observations upon which the book is based. They worked very hard, and I really cannot thank them enough. They clearly care a great deal about the next generation of Latino students and leaders.

Thank you, Cecilia "Ceci" Ceja, Melissa Dejesus, Jenny Deleon, Immaculada Figueroa, Jeanette Galindo, Citlay Gómez, Lucia Gonzalez, Guadalupe Jaimes, Ana Maradiaga, Nydia Perez, Felicia A. Ramos, Gardenia Rangel, Denisse Chapa-Malacara, and Josh Voit, the only non-Latino student involved with the research. I would also like to thank the staff of District 65 Family Focus, the social service agency that helped us identify and gain access to the families who allowed us to intrude upon their daily lives for so long. I hope that their forbearance and the efforts of the students will not be in vain, and that poor Latino and black students about whom we have been so concerned will not have to wait much longer for a better education. It is hoped that this research may help those who educate poor Latino and poor black students to improve the quality of that education through a greater focus on the family in the education process.

1

THE ISSUE

There is little doubt that inner-city schools, those schools attended for the most part by poor and working-class black and Latino children, are failing to adequately prepare their students for our highly complex and changing world. While this is not the case for all of the schools attended by poor blacks and Latinos, nor for all inner-city black and Latino students, it is nevertheless all too often the case. We have tried to solve this urgent problem by issuing school vouchers, forming charter schools, lengthening the school day, curbing social promotions, giving more standardized tests (on which poor blacks and Latinos do considerably worse than middle-income white students), requiring school uniforms, decentralizing school decision making, centralizing decision making, and more stringent requirements for both teachers and students. Still, as Traub (2000) writes, "Though over the past 35 years we have poured billions of dollars into inner-city schools, and though we have fiddled with practically everything you could think to fiddle with, we have done almost nothing to raise the trajectory of ghetto children" (p. 52).

Our efforts, while well intentioned, have not managed to significantly improve the quality of education offered to poor nonwhites or to help them do better. As I argue in my previous book (Sampson 2002), I believe that our lack of success here is due, to a significant degree, to the fact that we have focused upon school-based solutions and paid scant attention to the role of the most important institution in the developmental and educational process, the family. When educators discuss the role of the family in education, they typically start and stop with parental participation, as though coaxing poor nonwhite parents to PTA meetings will somehow miraculously change a poor Latino student doing poorly into one doing very well in school.

Some years ago I attended the parental conference for one of my daughters at her middle school. Although the enrollment was about 30 percent black, there was only one other black parent among the seventy or eighty gathered in the school cafeteria for that session. I waited for some twenty or thirty minutes until it was my turn and then met with the various teachers. The other black parent, who arrived before I did, was still waiting when I was about to leave. I wondered why she had not approached any teacher, and so I went up to her and asked. She indicated that she was afraid, intimidated by the teachers and the surroundings. I asked her name, reassured her as best I could, and left. I later asked my daughters whether they knew a student with her last name. Not only did they know the student, but she was one of the better students in the school. Here we had a black woman, who it turns out was also poor, who was apparently sending her daughter to school prepared to learn, who was too intimidated by the school to talk to the daughter's teachers at the parental conferences.

Would getting this lady to PTA meetings have made much difference? Not likely. The parents who might attend these meetings are those unlikely to be bothered by the very middle-class nature of our public schools and, I suspect, more likely than many others to do the things necessary at home for their children to perform better in school. I do not doubt that getting parents into schools might help some to figure out how to parent better, but not many. For the most part, those who are active are already doing what they need to do, so we are preaching to the converted.

Schools can be scary places for many poor folks. Teachers have degrees. They are well dressed. They have jobs. They are well spoken. Schools have schedules. They have order. Most poor folks have none of this. As Comer (1993) puts it, "The school is not a part of their social network. Their families often do not sense a right to be there and a oneness with the people and purpose of the school; and in a variety of ways the feeling is transmitted to the children" (p. 307). Schools are middle-class institutions both in their structure and in their desired output (Comer 1993; Sampson 2002). We should not be very surprised that they often fail to work well for those who are not middle class. I did not write "middle income," for social class and income, while related, are not really the same. Quite a few poor folks are middle class in their values, attitudes, and worldview, all of which are important to the educational process. For the most part, the children from these families perform at least reasonably well in school.

However, Comer (1993) also tells us, "The school is an instrument of the mainstream culture" (p. 305). This may be particularly problematic for those not steeped in that culture, and a number of Latinos would fall into this category. Given the growth of the Latino population in many of our major cities, including New York, Los Angeles, Dallas, Houston, Miami, Phoenix, and Chicago, I think that it makes sense to examine how poor Latino families prepare their children for school. Why poor Latinos? In 2002 I did the same research, focusing on poor blacks. Given that in many cities in which the poor do not do well in school, the body of poor students is largely black and Latino, it makes sense to try to determine what is going on in terms of education with the other group. This focus also allows some comparison with poor blacks.

When I write "what is going on in terms of education," I mean how the family prepares or fails to prepare the inner-city Latino or black student for school. To cite Comer (1993) again, "Development begins with the family. The family is enmeshed in and carries the attitudes, values, and ways of its social network" (p. 303). He continues, "Caretakers, then, are extremely powerful and in a position to greatly influence child development" (p. 303). Sigel (1985), Bempechat (1998), Clark (1983), and others also emphasize the primacy of the family in education. Yet, most research on school performance and almost all education policy aimed at improving the education of poor nonwhites is school based. That is, they aim to change schools, not families.

As I indicated above, many poor families do precisely what is needed to maximize the chances that their children will do well in school, often in the face of serious obstacles. Many others do not. I wanted to determine in this research the extent to which poor Latino families are doing these things, and I wanted to some extent to compare what poor Latino families are doing to what poor black families are doing. Unlike others, such as Joseph Viteritti, whose book *Choosing Equality* is often cited by voucher supporters, I do not believe that the failure of poor blacks and Latino as groups to perform well in public schools is an issue of equal opportunity. Not only do I believe that Viteritti is wrong when he asserts that this is the case, but I also believe that he is to some degree disingenuous.

Poor students have the opportunity to attend good schools. Because of the lack of money, they do not have the opportunity to attend costly private schools. However, these schools are not the ones in question. We need to improve the performance of poor nonwhite students in the schools that they overwhelmingly attend: inner-city public schools. The issue is not equality of opportunity but equality of outcome, the opportunity for a full life using an adequate education. Money does not ensure equal opportunity. There are plenty of suburban schools, and city schools with significant numbers of poor students, in which the per pupil expenditure is the same for all students and in which many poor nonwhite students perform significantly worse than their middle-income and white classmates. The same amount of money is being spent, but the outcome is not the same. I suspect that Viteritti is trying to justify the use of vouchers for nonpoor, white students at nonpublic schools and is using the disingenuous argument that the vouchers are designed to help poor nonwhites achieve equality of opportunity to support his case.

The question is, how do we bring about better outcomes for poor nonwhite students? Except for class size and preschool, money is not really the issue. Again, this assumes that schools have some basic level of facilities, commitment on the part of teachers and administrators, supplies, and commitment on the part of parents. This last is the problem—the parents, the families. It is not a problem for all poor nonwhite families, but for those for whom it is, we need to better understand precisely how it is and develop family-centered plans to deal with it. This is why I am focusing on poor Latino families, rather than on what schools do or do not do with poor Latino students.

While poor black students and poor Latino students face many of the same problems in public education, poor Latinos often face two additional problems: cultural differences and language differences. Black Americans grow up in the context of the American culture, and while many may not be completely absorbed in that culture, it is the only one to which they are exposed on a daily basis. They also grow up speaking only English, though some may well speak a version of that language that seems different to others. The reality is that middle-income blacks do not speak a different version and show no signs of a different culture, making it difficult to argue that blacks have either a different culture or a different language. If they did, even middle-income blacks would speak that language and absorb that culture. Those isolated from the rest of society may well be somewhat different, and their differences may well hold them back. Indeed, to some degree it is these differences that we seek to determine and understand so that they do not continue to stymie the success of poor nonwhite students. In this case I am looking for any real differences in the home environment that may limit the educational success of poor Latinos.

According to Herbert Grossman (1995), "The average achievement of Hispanic students is considerably lower than European American students at every grade level (5–14). By the eleventh and twelfth grades, while only 25.7 percent of European Americans have repeated at least one grade level, the corresponding figure for Hispanic students is 40.8; for Hispanic males the percentage is 54.2" (p. 5). He continues, "The results for students who are poor and Hispanic are especially discouraging. In comparison to middle class Hispanic students, they are even more likely to drop out of school, to achieve less while in school, and to earn lower grades" (p. 5, 6). Grossman attributes this lack of achievement to the clash between "the Hispanic culture" and "the European American culture," "the failure of schools to adapt to the contextual aspects of many Hispanic students' lives," and discrimination (p. 7).

Or as Darder, Torres, and Gutierrez (1997) put it, "Despite generations of protests, activism, and reform efforts, the historical record and current statistical data confirm the persistence of Latinos among the nation's most educationally disadvantaged and economically disenfranchised groups" (p. xii). There is, then, little doubt that poor Latino students as a group fare considerably worse in school than do nonpoor white students. The question is, why? We need to answer this question before we can move toward an effective solution. Clearly, if students do not speak English well and all instruction is in English, Latinos will have a serious problem (or is it that our society has the serious problem?). While there is no single Latino culture, and we all will do well to understand and remember that, many Latinos are steeped in cultures that are significantly different from both the culture of our public schools and the culture taught by those schools. That is another disadvantage. Then for many there is poverty. Still another disadvantage. Most efforts to improve the education offered to poor Latino students have focused upon the language and cultural differences, often ignoring the cultural differences within the Latino population. While language and culture must be considered, I believe that we will do well to consider the role of the family in preparing students for school, especially for those groups of students doing poorly in school.

As Edgar Epps writes so forcefully and eloquently in his foreword to Reginald Clark's book on the education of poor black families (1983): "The family is the basic institution through which children learn who they are, where they fit into society, and what kinds of futures they are likely to experience. One's ethnic group membership determines much of the content and flavor of interaction within the family. If one is black, Puerto Rican, or Chicano, he or she will be exposed to parental values and priorities that differ in important ways from those experienced by white children. Within each ethnic group, values and priorities are also influenced by the family's social status" (p. ix). It is my intention to try to examine and understand the values and priorities of a group of poor Latinos as they relate to the education of their children and to compare them to those of poor blacks.

While few scholars would deny the importance of the family in the educational process, there is surprisingly little work examining the precise values, attitudes, beliefs, and behavior of families as they relate to children's education. Most of the work examining the link between families and success in life focuses on characteristics such as family size, number of siblings, number of intact families, occupational and educational status of parents, and parental expectations of the child's academic success (Coleman et al. 1966; Blau and Duncan 1967). While helpful, these studies fail to examine the details of the family dynamic or the values, attitudes, and behavior that may largely determine whether a child is sent to school prepared to learn and therefore in a position to perform better.

Clark (1983), Bempechat (1998), Furstenberg et al. (1999), and Sampson (2002) rely on ethnographic research techniques (though all but Sampson also make extensive use of questionnaires) to determine precisely what things parents do and do not do every day that help determine their children's readiness for the educational experience. This book focuses more upon values, attitudes, and worldview as they are shaped by the parents in their interaction with the children than upon what Clark (1983) refers to as "surface status characteristics" (p. 6) such as the education, occupation, and income of the parents. These variables do indeed play a role in the development of the child and therefore in the child's education. However, when the families are all poor, all have roughly the same occupational status, educational background, race or ethnicity, why are some children better prepared for school than others? This is a more complicated question, and it is the question that I seek to answer in this work with poor and working-class Latinos.

What I found in my earlier work, which is supported to some considerable degree by the work of Clark (1983), Furstenberg et al. (1999), Comer (1993), and others, is that poor black families in which the children perform well in school tend to be families in which the children are taught discipline, positive self-esteem, cooperation, internal control, high educational aspirations, a focus on the future, and a sense of responsibility. The home environments of these students are orderly, structured, and quiet, allowing for homework, discussion with parents, and teaching of positive personal characteristics. In this work I want to determine the degree to which poor and working-class Latino families stress the same characteristics of the children and of the home environment.

A LATINO DIFFERENCE?

According to Comer (1993), "Schools are instruments of the mainstream culture.... Children from social networks with similar attitudes, values, and ways to those of the school and the most powerful school people have the best opportunity to meet the expectations of the school" (p. 305). He cites the work of Sara Lightfoot (1978) to support this critical argument. Essentially the argument is that those students raised in middle-class homes to be middle-class students will perform better than others in school. I have found this to be on target where poor black students are concerned. However, Grossman (1995) argues that Latino students are culturally different from non-Latinos and from other Latino students from different Spanish-speaking countries. If this is true, many Latino students would have a serious problem with school that many other students do not have; they are not

necessarily a part of, or steeped in, the mainstream culture and would therefore be at a considerable disadvantage when it comes to education in that
culture. I am not going to get involved in the debate over whether the mainstream culture should or should not adapt or be more flexible to accommodate these students.

To the degree that cultural differences influence what things are done
and how they are done, I will point this out. While 71 percent of the Latino
respondents in Grossman's survey (1995) think that there is a "Latin American culture" in the United States, 61 percent of them believe that the differences between the Latin American culture and the non-Hispanic cultures
are due mostly to economic differences rather than actual cultural differences. I make the same argument concerning the differences between blacks
and nonblacks. What is seen by some as a black culture is in reality a
"ghetto" culture, and in reality many poor blacks in the ghetto are not a part
of this culture, and their children often manage to do just fine in school and
in life, in large measure because the school is an instrument of the larger,
middle-class culture.

Bempechat (1998) does in fact suggest that Latinos have a different approach to education than blacks, having what she terms a "collectivist orientation toward child rearing" that stresses academic achievement but
causes the students to feel guilty about the sacrifices made by the parents in
the students' pursuit of a good education. Grossman (1995) refers to this as
stressing the importance of the group and the extended family. He argues
that this causes Latino students to be more cooperative and group oriented
than Anglo students and to want to work more closely with other students
to demonstrate their helpfulness and generosity. Latinos, according to
Grossman, emphasize cooperation over competition and do not want
to embarrass others by doing better in individual achievement. They are
taught to share and to respect their elders, characteristics that may be related to an unwillingness to state disagreements with others, especially
those who are older and more experienced. He also argues that "the Hispanic culture tends to be patriarchal" (p. 127), which may result in male
students having difficulty taking direction from female teachers.

It does not appear to me that these characteristics, to the degree that they
are in fact accurate, would conflict with those of successful poor minority
students or of their homes that I noted earlier. My earlier work with poor

black families found that the father played virtually no role in preparing the student for school. It should be interesting to see the role played by Latino fathers, given the emphasis on the male that some scholars point out in the Latino culture. While some of these characteristics may have implications for teaching style and approach, I do not see that they seriously affect the characteristics shown by successful poor minority students. Still, it is best to be sensitive to overgeneralization.

If the Latino family is as important to Latino students as Grossman indicates, then we must pay considerable attention to what these families do and do not do to prepare their children for school. How helpful are the parents in terms of schoolwork? How encouraging are they? Do they maintain a home environment that is conducive to studying and concentrating on schoolwork? Do they have high educational expectations of the students, and do they transmit those expectations to their children? Do they engage in activities that promote a sense of responsibility on the part of the student? In the case of preschool children, are the parents engaged in the kinds of activities shown by research to have a positive impact upon the child's learning ability, such as talking to the child, reading to the child, and helping the child? These are all critical questions if we are to understand the role played by families in the educational process.

Of course, we must be sensitive to the role of language in much of this. For example, how can a parent who speaks little English help a sixth grader with a social studies assignment written in English? Helping the child answer questions is not really the key here. What is important is that the child learns from the importance the parent assigns to the work that the work should be important to the child and that the child must take seriously the work and the responsibility to do it. After all, if the parent can take the time to work with the child, the work must be important. But if the parent is deterred by the language difference, the child may not get the message.

FRAMING THE ISSUES

"The involvement of parents in the education of their school-age children is probably the greatest single opportunity for educational advance open to us today" (Hurst 1996, 105). This involvement goes well beyond what we have traditionally thought of as "parental involvement." It is much more than attendance at PTA meetings or parent-teacher conferences, though this attendance may well be correlated with the kinds of activities, attitudes, and behavior engaged in by those parents who send their children to school prepared to learn.

This research seeks to examine just how poor Latino parents prepare their children for school. The work of Furstenberg et al. (1999), Sampson (2002), Bempechat (1998), Clark (1983), and Grossman (1995) clearly indicates that many poor parents are quite concerned with the education of their children. Interest and concern are not the issues. The question is how this concern is translated into the attitudes, values, and behavior necessary for the child to perform well in school. That is, how do some poor parents manage to prepare their children for schools, which are inherently middle-class institutions?

Most of the discussion on improving public education for poor minority students has focused on changes in the school and its employees. This focus is, I believe, in many cases misplaced. While schools must be adequately staffed, have necessary supplies and equipment, and have staff members who believe in their students, it is the family, the home, from which the needed values, beliefs, and attitudes must come. Hurst (1996) is correct when she suggests that the family offers the greatest opportunity for educational improvement. It is not that improvement cannot come from changes in school. For the greatest possible improvement, however, I believe that we must look to families and homes, specifically those of poor minority students in urban areas.

In Chicago, students who attend chronically underperforming schools have the right to transfer to other schools. That is nice, but what happens to the schools from which these students transfer? The students who transfer are likely to be those whose parents not only care very much about their children's education but also have the knowledge and initiative to make the change. In other words, they are likely to be to some degree middle-class parents who happen to be poor. When these students leave the schools, they leave behind an even higher percentage of students who need to learn to emulate them. While I certainly do not believe that these students should stay to set the example for others, their leaving will not help the former school to improve and may in fact not help the students themselves much, since middle-class students are likely to do better wherever they are.

Milwaukee has hitched its educational star to vouchers, even though Lieberman (1993) tells us that "there is no evidence that the Milwaukee public schools have changed since the voucher plan became operative" (p. 13). Other school systems are focusing upon charter schools as the answer. But Michael Winerip (1998) tells us that the real difference between charter schools and others is the motivation of the parents of the charter school students. Again, the issue is parents and what they do and do not do. Longer school years are being tried despite the research indicating that this has no impact upon performance (Berliner and Biddle 1995). More tests, fewer tests, more-stringent requirements for teachers, school uniforms are all being tried, but none has yet shown that it helps poor minority students do significantly better in school. We talk about spending more money on the schools attended by these students even though we have known for some time that money affects education in basically only two ways: lowering class size to roughly sixteen to seventeen students per class, and providing preschool education. There is not much talk in areas with large numbers of poor minority students about tripling the budget to accommodate these changes.

I am suggesting, not that we give up on school reform, but that we try to realize just how limited school change may be and how large an improvement may be at hand in terms of the role of the family and the home. On a nice, warm spring day most students would rather be outside playing or talking than sitting in a stuffy classroom listening to a stuffed-shirt teacher discuss algebra or Chaucer. Yet, many sit there quietly, absorbing this mostly irrelevant information. Why? Because they like Chaucer? Unlikely. They do it because they are disciplined, and because they can delay gratification. That is, they can put off the immediate pleasure of playing on a nice day for the longer-term payoff that comes from a good education. Where do they get the discipline and the ability to delay gratification? They certainly are not born with them. No, they learn them (or they do not) at home; and if they learn them, they are likely to perform better in school than those who do not.

I wanted to study poor Latino families in order to find out just what the children in these families are (or are not) learning from their parents and homes that might affect how well they can do in school and, to some degree, to compare these families with the poor black families I studied recently. The goal is to add to our knowledge of poor black and Latino families so that we might improve the education offered to them. I suspect that much of this improvement will have to take place at home.

2

RESEARCH METHODS

A s in my previous work on the education of poor black students, I have relied basically upon an ethnographic, observational methodology, in this
case focusing upon observations of the everyday lives and daily interactions of
the members of eight poor Latino families and the twenty-one children in
those families. My earlier work on poor black families (2002) examined the
lives, values, and attitudes of twelve poor black families and focused upon one
child in each family. The original goal was to replicate the earlier work with
poor Latinos, but two circumstances made that goal impractical. First, a number of the parents who wanted to participate in the study had preschool children, while the earlier study focused on older children, those in grades 5
through 9. This of course made the examination of academic achievement as
a result of the attitudes and values ingrained at home almost impossible given
that I had no measure of achievement for the preschoolers.

Second, it was more difficult to find families who were willing to allow
observers into their homes for hours at a time over two months. While this
was not at all easy in the case of poor blacks, a number of them had very
close ties to a local community organization, Family Focus, that helped with
the work. These ties enabled us to work with a few more families. In the
case of my research on Latinos, the community organization with which
I worked, another Family Focus office, did not seem to have the same strong
relationships with families. Also, perhaps some of the poor Latinos were

even more distrustful of this kind of intervention than were poor blacks. This makes sense given that all but two of the parents were from Mexico; one was from Peru, and one from Nicaragua. These are not families who have spent their entire lives in America.

Gaining the trust of poor families, which is necessary if one is to spend a lot of time in their homes, is not easy. The support of the community organization is essential. Because we were observing over time, I was not overly concerned with the possibility that the parents or the children would change their behavior owing to the presence of the observer. While such changes might take place, they are difficult to maintain over hours or weeks. While this research methodology allows us to examine the family dynamic in depth, it limits the number of families that may be observed. We have longer looks at the families, but fewer families at which we can look. The best way to minimize the impact of this limitation is to study the families over time. This work does just that, while adding the variable of ethnicity, and allows comparisons between Latinos and blacks.

Clark (1983) found when he began his ethnographic research, the usual mood of the families that he wanted to observe was "What government agency does he work for?" or "I thought you was the police" (p. 19). For a variety of reasons, it may well be that some Latinos believe even more strongly than many poor blacks that they should be very careful with strangers in their homes. Clark studied ten poor black families, and Furstenberg (1997) studied fifteen families, some Latino, some Anglo, and some black, some working class, some poor, and some lower middle income. As I have indicated, in my earlier work I studied twelve poor black families. This study seeks to build upon the work of Clark, Furstenberg, and my earlier research.

In any research that is as invasive as this work is, the trust of the families being studied is critical. They are, after all, allowing unknown observers into their homes for hours at a time over several weeks—observers may well see and hear things that families normally keep private and that could be embarrassing. This is one reason that the support of the community agency is critical. The families trust the staff of the agency, with whom they have worked over time, and when the staff members indicate that the observers can be trusted, this opens the door for them. In this case all of the observers were themselves Latino. I decided that this was the only way to proceed with this research not only because it was critical that the observers speak fluent Spanish, given that most of the families were likely to speak Spanish at home, but also because I thought that observers steeped in Latino culture could better understand what they heard and observed.

Family Focus is a well-established community agency based in Evanston, Illinois, a diverse community just north of Chicago. It works to improve the quality of life for poor families, especially children, in Evanston. This office of Family Focus is located in an area of Evanston in which a number of poor Latino families live; its client base is about 50 percent Latino. I selected families in Evanston for several reasons. First, I initially wanted to replicate my earlier study on poor black students in Evanston. Second, selecting Evanston allowed us to rule out significant differences among the schools attended as a factor. Finally, the focus on Evanston allows us to rule out, or at least minimize, the impact of significant differences in neighborhood on preparing children for school. I believe that the neighborhood in which one lives may affect the way one raises a child, since the neighborhood may provide unique limitations and opportunities.

While these differences in parenting and school preparation may of course be taken into account in the analysis of data, this generally will require a larger sample, and given the invasive nature of this research, a large sample would be problematic.

The population of Evanston according to the 2000 census is 74,239, or 1,006 more than in 1990. In 1990, Latinos constituted 3 percent of the total population; in 2000, the figure had risen to 6.1 percent. The black population fell from 22.9 percent of the total in 1990 to 22.5 percent in 2000. The bulk of the Latino population resides in the southern part of the city, the section served by the office of Family Focus with which I worked. About 15 percent of both the black and Latino populations are below the poverty line.

The neighborhoods occupied largely by Latinos and blacks are also the poorer neighborhoods and those with the higher incidences of crime (Sampson 2002). Evanston has two school systems: an elementary school system and a high school system, which is essentially three schools housed in one building. The high schools are attended by all public school students.

THE SAMPLE

Working with Family Focus, we found eight families who were interested in participating in the study or, should I say, were willing to allow us to invade their privacy for seven to eight weeks. I cannot overemphasize the difficulty involved in persuading families, particularly immigrant families in which folks often speak relatively little English, to allow observers who are strangers to sit in their homes for hours at a time and listen to their conversations, watch their actions, and report them to another researcher. So, the sample size is small, but the data rich. Obviously, the size of the sample limits the generalizability of the research. However, the methodology practically dictates a small sample. Because I have very recently done the same kind of work with a sample of poor blacks in the same city (Sampson 2002), and because others such as Bempechat (1998), Clark (1983), and, to a lesser extent, Furstenberg et al. (1999) have used the same methodology very effectively, I believe I am in a position to shed considerable light upon what poor non-white families do and do not do that effectively prepares their children for school success.

I believe that the intense, time-consuming ethnographic technique is best for this subject. More research of this type will allow greater confidence in the outcomes, but the data are certainly building. In this case the eight families had a total of twenty-one children, ranging in age from one year old to thirteen years old. All eight of the families have a husband present, which is quite different from the poor black families that I studied. Fourteen of the parents came from Mexico, one came from Peru, and one from Nicaragua.

The backgrounds of the families, together with the ages of the children, present unique challenges given the research technique. We had to be particularly sensitive to language and cultural differences. A gesture by someone raised in the United States may well have a different meaning, or no meaning at all, for a person raised in Mexico. Of course, the observers not only had to know Spanish but also understand any differences in Hispanic and U.S. culture. Further, the range in the ages of the children meant that we had to pay attention to any differences in the dealings with the children that might have been the effect of age as opposed to differences in child preparation. Clark (1983), Bempechat (1998), and Sampson (2002) all studied school-aged students and concentrated on students from middle to high school.

Having preschoolers in the sample required us to pay attention to any differences in the relationship between parents and those preschoolers that might affect their schooling later. Preschoolers, for example, do not typically do homework, so I could not look for the ways parents deal with children and homework. Further, only the students in middle or high school in Evanston have letter grades. Below the sixth grade the teachers indicate whether a student's performance in the different skill areas are strong, acceptable, or require improvement. This makes the comparison of grades for students below the sixth grade very difficult, if not meaningless. Only two students in the sample were in middle school, eight were of preschool age, and none were in high school. There were ten boys and eleven girls. Therefore, only two students had letter grades to compare, and they were both in the same family.

Thus, instead of comparing the families by the grades of the children, I had to compare them in terms of what they do and do not do in terms of those behaviors that we know from earlier work have a positive impact on school performance. I should note that while the observers collected the data for this study, I alone performed the data analysis. The observers had no input into the analysis process.

As discussed in chapter 1, the work of Clark (1983), Furstenberg et al. (1999), and Sampson (2002), as well as Harrington and Boardman (1997), suggests a number of characteristics that seem to be present in the homes and families of those who do well in school and in this society. Those who perform well are disciplined, have high self-esteem, have the ability to cooperate, are internally controlled, have a future orientation, have a sense of responsibility, have high educational aspirations, and live in an orderly, structured, and quiet home environment. Actually, these would appear to be characteristics of middle-class or, as Comer (1993) might refer to them, "mainstream" families. This is why I suggest that some poor families are in fact middle class in terms of values, attitudes, and beliefs.

COLLECTING THE DATA

The staff at Family Focus introduced me and nine observers to a number of Latino families with whom they work and asked me to explain the purposes and methods of the study. Of these families, eight agreed to participate. All observations took place in the homes of the participants while at least some of the children in each family were present. This allowed us to observe the family dynamic particularly in terms of the interaction of parents and children that might influence the child's success in school. The observers met with the families for two to three hours a day, once or twice a week, for six to eight weeks. Scheduling was not always easy, given the complexity of the lives of poor and working-class families.

The observers were trained to observe almost everything about family life, and we focused on family structure, home environment, and family processes. We observed interaction, intervention, responsibilities, values, and attitudes. We looked at such issues as self-esteem, locus of control, and whether education was valued, and we observed educational processes within the family: Does the parent help the child with schoolwork? Does the parent encourage and motivate the child? Does the parent stimulate the preschool child?

The observers made notes after each visit and submitted them to me. I then suggested changes in the approaches as necessary. In addition, we used questionnaires to gather background information about the parents, the children, and the attitudes and behavior of the parent responding to the questionnaire regarding schools and education (see appendix). We administered questionnaires to the older children as well to assess some of their attitudes and feelings, especially regarding education.

As Comer (1993) writes: "They [parents] celebrate different holidays in particular ways. They value or do not value the arts, schooling, timeliness, disciplined behavior, and so on. Living with their parents, children are acculturated to the attitudes, values, and ways of their social network or subculture. Children from all social networks and/or subcultures then go off to school" (p. 305). The question is, how well are they prepared in terms of values, attitudes, and behavior for that mainstream, middle-class school experience? Many poor parents prepare their children well, despite the common perception that poor minority children are seldom prepared. Let us now examine the degree to which poor Latino parents prepare their children for school. In the chapters that follow, I have changed the names of family members to protect their privacy.

It should also be noted that the observers and I were introduced to the families by the Family Focus staff prior to the start of the observations. At this meeting, I explained the purposes of the research and the research process. In most cases the questionnaires were administered during the first observation, but in others, the observers felt that it was better to wait until some degree of rapport had been established before asking the questions. For the most part, the analysis for each family begins with the data collected from the questionnaires.

3

THE FAMILIES

THE CEJAS

Eva Ceja lives with her husband and four children in Evanston; she grew up in Mexico City. Her husband works in the maintenance department of a local institution, "fixing things around the department, such as replacing light bulbs, broken windows, etc." He is also from Mexico City and completed level 3 of schooling, which is about eleven years of school in Mexico, and beyond secondary education there. Eva herself went two years beyond level 3. She says that the education of her children was her "priority," and was the main reason why she and her husband migrated to America. When asked whether she encouraged her four children to do well in school, she replied, "Of course I do." According to Ms. Ceja, she does this by "giving them the time they need for their work. Give them time and space. Help whenever they have problems." She indicated that she visits the school of the three who are in school once or twice a month.

When she visits the school, however, she said that she feels "incompetent, frustrated, uncomfortable, and angry." She sees too much aggression in the schools, and she sees racism and discrimination as well. Clearly, according to Ms. Ceja, she shows the kind of concern for, and involvement in, the education of her children that educators suggest is critical if they are to do their jobs well. She visits their school, helps with the homework, and gives them the space and time they need to do the schoolwork. She seems also to be quite aware of what is going on in the school, noting the aggression and the racism. This does not appear to be a poor minority parent who is uninvolved with her children's education, at least not based upon what she says. Entwisle, Alexander, and Olson (1997), Comer (1993), and others indicate that the involvement of parents in the education of their children, both in school and in the home, is very important to the educational success of the students. While this kind of involvement is standard for middle-class parents, many poor parents, especially immigrants, may be intimidated by the teachers and/or the school environment and therefore fail to involve themselves with the school. However, many poor parents, like Ms. Ceja, are indeed willing to be involved and in this and other important ways they are in fact middle class.

When asked "What, if anything, stands in [Natalie's or Eloise's] way in terms of getting a good education?" Ms. Ceja answered, "In general, I do not see that every teacher cares about their students' education. Each student is different and needs different things." She continued, "Hispanic students are at a disadvantage. They do not have the same opportunities, whether this is because of economic situation, racism, (or what)." Clearly, this is an observant parent, a parent who believes that the educational system is not doing its job well enough. Yet, she has indicated that she moved here for her children to receive a better education. Does she expect too much?

Ms. Ceja indicated that other children do not attempt to stop her two children in school from doing well. I asked this question because some scholars, such as Fordham and Ogbu (1986), have suggested that, for poor blacks at least, academic accomplishment is seen by others as "acting white" and is therefore to be avoided. The idea is that some may limit their own accomplishments in order to be accepted by the group that wants to avoid "acting white" (as though whites have a corner on academic achievement), while others may try to pressure classmates into limiting their achievement both because it is "white" and because it may show up those who are doing poorly.

Grossman (1995) touches upon this issue within the context of what he sees as Latino culture. Instead of "acting white" it is called "sofisticado," or acting as though one is better than others, which might lead students to limit themselves or to attempt to limit others. The data in Grossman's work are not clear on whether this pressure really exists.

But Ms. Ceja does believe that Natalie and Eloise's French teacher hinders their achievement because "she does not know how to control or handle different situations. She disrespects her students and they in turn disrupt her." Clearly, this is a woman paying attention to the education process. Whether she is right or wrong is not the issue. The point is that she pays enough attention to the education being offered to her daughters that she has come to the conclusion that their French teacher cannot control her class. Again, this is not the image that we typically have of a poor or working-class nonwhite parent who cares very little, and knows even less, about the education of her children.

Ms. Ceja said that race and/or discrimination "definitely" plays a role in her life. She cited the "language barrier," "everyday life," and her "husband's job" as examples. She is sensitive to what she perceives to be discrimination against her.

When asked to describe her upbringing, Ms. Ceja said of her parents, "They taught me many things. They taught me to respect everyone, especially my elders. They taught me how to be civilized—something that is not always taught here. They always supported me in every aspect of my personal and school life." Grossman (1995) mentions that Latino children are taught to respect their elders, and Ms. Ceja has now mentioned the issue of respect twice. In fact, she went on to say that she wants to raise her children the same way that she was raised and that she wants to "teach them respect." It may well be that respect is very important to Latinos and that individual achievement at almost any cost, which seems to drive many Americans, is at odds with this respect for others. If so, some Latino students maybe suffer a disadvantage in school that has nothing to do with ability or interest but with the way they are raised. This bears watching as we look at the other families.

Ms. Ceja said she never reads the newspaper, but she reads a book every day. It will be interesting to see how often she reads to her preschool children, given the importance of reading to preschoolers as preparation for school. She indicated that when she has a problem she can rely upon "no one," since "good friends are not abundant here." She relies upon "only God." A number of the poor black families that I studied also indicated that they rely on God when they have a problem. Is this a sign of external control? We shall revisit this issue as we look at more of the families and compare them to the black families.

Ms. Ceja believes that everyone who wants to get ahead in America and really tries can do so. This suggests that she believes that the future is in the hands of individuals and that hard work is all it takes. This would suggest internal control and a belief that despite the discrimination that she believes exists and plays a role in her life, achievement is possible. This is not a woman sitting around waiting for things to happen or one who believes that things are preordained and therefore effort is not rewarded. She seems to believe that anything is possible with hard work, and this of course is a good belief to pass on to her children. Does she do this, and how?

We also interviewed both Eloise and Natalie. Eloise is a thirteen-year-old seventh grader at a kindergarten-through-eighth-grade school in an area of Evanston that has been historically black but is becoming more and more Latino and black. Natalie is a twelve-year-old sixth grader at the same school. When asked what she most liked about her school, Eloise replied, "Ms. Davis and her friends. She's a fun science teacher. We do a lot of experiments and I learn in that class. If I don't understand something or am too embarrassed to ask something in front of the class, she always helps me and makes me understand." When asked what she least likes about the school, she indicated that it was the assistant principal because "he doesn't believe me—ever. Everything I say is a lie to him. He is always getting me in trouble, and he's a racist." It is actually unlikely that the assistant principal is getting her into trouble and more likely that she is getting herself into trouble and that the assistant principal is not giving her a break.

More important, when asked how well she is doing in school, she answered, "Poorly," and when asked how important education was to her, she replied, "Not at all important." These answers suggest that she may well not be a good student and lead me to wonder just what her parents are doing in the home to properly prepare her for school and for that education that her mother seems to believe is so important that they migrated from Mexico to Evanston. Indeed, Eloise said, "I just don't care [about school]. Besides, I'm gonna get an F in all of my classes even if I try." She appears to be a poor student with little motivation to perform well, despite what her mother says about the importance of education. Most parents, however, say that the education of their children is important to them. The issue is how this importance gets translated into actions in the home that convince the children of the importance and properly prepare them for the school experience.

According to Eloise, no one has attempted to prevent her from doing well in school. But why should they if she is doing as poorly as she indicates? She said that she spends half an hour to an hour during the week and no time at all on the weekends on homework. This contrasts with the two to three hours a day devoted to homework by the better poor black students in the Evanston middle school that I studied recently (Sampson 2002). When asked how far she would like to go in school, Eloise said that she expects to complete the first year of high school. The better poor black students often indicated that they wanted to attend graduate school.

So, here we have a student doing poorly in school, by her own admission; she seems to get into a fair amount of trouble in school and has very low educational expectations. She does not appear to be a student adequately prepared for school by her parents. When asked what obstacles were in her way in terms of doing well in school, she indicated that adults "just don't think that I can do it. They say I'm stupid. My friends that are not in school sometimes ask me to be with them and miss school. They taught me how to pick locks and car wires." These answers suggest that Eloise has low self-esteem and low expectations, when high self-esteem and high expectations are characteristics of higher-performing students and middle-class students. Her mother seems to have fairly high expectations of Eloise, but she does not seem to manage to transfer those to Eloise or to boost her self-esteem.

Like her mother, Eloise "never" reads a newspaper. When asked, "What is most important to you in your life," she answered, "Nothing. Nothing at all. It used to be David, but not anymore." It seems then that Eloise is also somewhat fatalistic or externally controlled. She shows none of the characteristics of a higher-achieving student or of a student who is sent to school by her parents prepared to learn. In fact, she said that her parents "never" help her with her schoolwork, and we know from earlier work that having parents help with schoolwork is very important because it demonstrates to the student the importance of that work and therefore of school. If schoolwork is important enough that parents take the time from their busy schedules to help, then it must be important, and the child learns this lesson. Apparently, Eloise has not learned it, though she says that her parents do not offer her enough help, suggesting that she would like more involvement from them.

When we asked Eloise, "If you could change one thing about your family life, what would it be?" her answer was, "Everyone's attitude against me. I'm always getting blamed . . . always getting compared. Today was my friend's birthday. They [her parents] say that if I keep going the way I am, I'm going to end up like her." The friend, as we shall see later, had a tragic end to her young life. It appears, then, that many of the characteristics known to be important for school achievement and greatly influenced by parents—positive self-esteem, high educational expectations, discipline, internal control, the ability to delay gratification—are missing in the case of Eloise, at least judging from what she says. The key now is to determine through the observations what role her parents play in her development, or lack thereof. But first, let us examine the answers to the questions posed to Natalie, Eloise's twelve-year-old sister.

Natalie is in the sixth grade at the same school attended by her older sister. While Eloise likes most about school her science teacher, Natalie seems to like all of the teachers. "They're nice and they teach very well." They both, however, dislike the assistant principal. Like Eloise, Natalie asserts that he is racist. She indicated that she is doing well in school and that her education is "very important" to her "because it's your future. It determines what job you get. It's everything." Education, then, seems to be more important to Natalie than to her sister, who is only one year older. It will be interesting to see just how it is that these two sisters so close in age seem to be so different when it comes to school performance, interest in education, and belief in the value of education. What role, if any, does the family play in shaping these differences?

Like her sister, Natalie indicated that no other student has tried to keep her from doing well in school. Also like her sister, she spends "a half hour . . . sometimes" on her homework during the week. "I usually finish it at school because it's very easy. If I have a big project to do, then I spend like two hours a day on it." It appears that Natalie is more dedicated to her schoolwork than Eloise and is willing to devote more time to it. However, even she does not spend the time on that work that the good poor black students do.

While Eloise expects to complete a year of high school, Natalie wants "to finish college." Indeed, she expects to finish college. She said, however, that her father tells her that if she is going to be a college teacher, "then I have to go for like two or more years after college. If I have to do that for my career, I will." Clearly, she has high academic expectations, much higher than those of her sister. She appears to be a very different young lady from her sister, especially in terms of those characteristics that are so important to academic performance. Yet, they live in the same household and are raised by the same parents.

Natalie sees no obstacles in the way of her achievement (after we explained just what "obstacles" means) and thinks that her family is the most important thing in her life. When asked whether race or racial discrimination was something about which she thinks very much, she replied, "No. Only if I'm in a fight because they say 'dirty Mexican.' But that usually doesn't happen because I don't get into fights." So Natalie must live with the racial taunts of other children in this highly diverse city.

While Eloise said that her parents never help her with her schoolwork, Natalie said that they help her a lot and that if she needs help with a big project, they help "like every day." "I only ask for help if I really don't understand something, then I ask my mom." So, it is the mother upon whom Natalie relies for help with her homework, but she also indicated that her father helped her recently with a big geography project. In the case of the poor black students, a father was present in the home in only half of the families and almost never did he participate in school-related activities with the child.

In fact, Natalie thinks that sometimes her parents help her "too much." But it is precisely this willingness on the part of parents to involve themselves in the academic work of their children that helps to teach them the value and importance of education. The question here is, why do the parents help Natalie so much and never help Eloise? It may be that the Cejas are willing to help the child who is doing well and not the other child. If this is true, perhaps their priorities, while understandable, are wrong. Of course, it could be that the child doing well is doing so in part because of the participation of the family. The question then is, why work with one child and not the other? The observations should help us understand these issues better. When asked what one thing she would change about her family life, Natalie complained about her seven-year-old brother, Devin. "He's always loud and always getting us in trouble. If he would just change his whole attitude, I wouldn't mind him." This bears watching.

The initial observation of the Ceja family took place at Family Focus. The staff invited a number of the families with whom they worked to meet with me and the observers to hear about the project and to match up with observers if they were interested in participating. The observer for the Ceja family noticed immediately that "most of the mothers there did not speak proper Spanish. They mispronounced or misused words, and had diverse accents." Ms. Ceja, however, "spoke very clear, precise, and grammatically correct Spanish, and she had a very extensive vocabulary," perhaps a reflection of her greater education.

Ms. Ceja indicated early in the initial conversation that she and her husband were having difficulty with Eloise, who in the past had been a good student but had lost interest in school and paid no attention to their efforts to turn her around. She indicated that she asks Eloise whether she has completed her homework, and Eloise always says that she has, but Ms. Ceja receives notes from her teachers stating that she has not done the work.

Ms. Ceja thinks that at age thirteen Eloise should be responsible enough to do the work on her own but that since she is not, she must always be "on her back." She went on to say that in her home certain things are done at certain times. She picks up the three school-age children from school (they all attend the same school), picks up her husband from work, and goes home to eat dinner. The children are then given time to relax before turning to their homework. After completing their homework, they can watch television or play with their friends. One of the characteristics of the homes of poor blacks in which students perform well noted by both Clark (1983) and myself (2002) is that home life is organized. That is, certain things are done at certain times day after day. Another is that the good students have a sense of responsibility. Indeed, students must have this sense of responsibility if they are to do well (Comer 1993). It appears that Ms. Ceja has an organized household, at least based upon what she says, and that she encourages responsibility on the part of her children.

However, the better poor black students whom I studied rarely watch television or play during the week. Their evenings are filled with homework (two to three hours a night), family chores, and extracurricular activities. The chores and extracurricular activities help build a sense of discipline and responsibility, both essential to good academic performance, and the extracurricular activities also help boost self-esteem, also important if a child is to do well in school.

Ms. Ceja discussed the tragic case of one of Eloise's very good friends who had recently committed suicide. This suicide had apparently seriously affected Eloise for several weeks, causing her to be upset and depressed, but she had recovered, according to her mother. Ms. Ceja had prohibited Eloise from playing with this girl, who, by the way, was black, because she believed that the girl was not a good influence on Eloise. Ms. Ceja based this opinion on an incident that took place in front of her house one day. The girl and her grandmother were walking past the Ceja home when the girl stopped to talk with Eloise. When the grandmother asked the girl to hurry, the girl yelled and screamed at her. Ms. Ceja then forbade Eloise to be her friend, telling her that the girl had different beliefs and customs than they had. While it is clear from this story that the girl had shown a lack of respect for an elder, which would have been a problem in many Latino households, it is not clear what the comment about different customs and beliefs was about. If it was racially based, it would be most interesting, since Evanston prides itself upon being very racially tolerant and both of the Ceja daughters mention racial discrimination against themselves. Are they being taught discrimination by their mother?

When Eloise told her mother that she assumed that she would not be allowed to attend the girl's funeral, Ms. Ceja told her that not only could she attend but that Ms. Ceja would go with her, explaining that what the girl did or did not do was not her fault. She was raised by her grandmother because "she did not have parents to raise her. It was not her fault that she did not know right from wrong. She was just a victim." This suggests that Ms. Ceja puts a great deal of weight upon familial responsibility to teach and guide children. She went on to say that she must approve all of Eloise's friends and that if they are going to the show, an adult must go with them. While this may seem rather strict for a thirteen-year-old today, Furstenberg et al. (1999), Clark (1983), and Sampson (2002) have found that a characteristic of the families of poor children who do well is this kind of strictness, almost rigidity, on the part of the parents. Still, Eloise does very poorly in school.

Ms. Ceja believes that Eloise must balance the differences in the customs and traditions at home and school, though speaking English is not a problem since she has attended school in Evanston since prekindergarten, certainly long enough for her to pick up the customs of the school. This is a key point. Obviously, if there are great differences in customs and traditions between home and school, a child may have difficulty in school. However, in the case of the Ceja family, Ms. Ceja did not mention Natalie, who is apparently doing well, when discussing these differences. Perhaps even more important is the question of whether Eloise should really have to choose or balance those customs or traditions if she is in fact being prepared for a world in which the public school is asked to impart the traditions, customs, and knowledge necessary for success in that world. If Ms. Ceja wants Eloise to be successful in America (and she says that this is the reason that she and her husband migrated here), it may well be that she should want her to master those customs and traditions offered through the school system, even though this requires a difficult balancing act on the part of the student, a difficulty of which educators should be aware. This is not an easy issue, and I will have to come back to it often, I suspect.

Ms. Ceja explained that they lack the financial resources to reward Natalie for her good grades as they would like, but she said that she and her husband have explained to Natalie that they understand and appreciate how hard she works and they wish they had the money to reward her. This kind of parental encouragement is important both in raising the student's self-esteem and in helping the student understand the value of work and of education. She and her husband do, however, use verbal rewards. Ms. Ceja said that since her English is limited, she relies on Natalie for some tasks and that Natalie for the most part does what she is told but occasionally questions why Eloise does not do very much. The importance of the tasks cannot be overemphasized. As I have already indicated, they build discipline, cooperation, and a sense of responsibility, all important to academic success.

Eloise, though, does not seem to have these responsibilities, for whatever reasons. Perhaps she does not accept them, or perhaps she is not given them by her parents because they feel that she will not accept them. Still, she does not have something that is important in terms of family preparation for school success, and her sister does. It is also important to note that Ms. Ceja indicated that her English is not very good. This would make dealing with school personnel, and perhaps school issues, somewhat difficult for her. She may also be at a disadvantage in terms of helping her children with their schoolwork, which is very important to their success.

Little is mentioned during this first visit about seven-year-old Devin or three-year-old Dennis, except that Devin apparently has trouble staying still and must keep busy. Ms. Ceja indicated that she reads to Dennis a great deal, but I suspect that this is done in Spanish. If so, the impact of this critical activity for preschoolers may be lessened. According to Stein (1986), reading is a very important part of the expectations of school. Comer (1993) notes that "mainstream," or what I term middle-class, parents read to their very young children, helping the child considerably when it comes time for school. Ms. Ceja did say that she wishes that she spoke English better so that she could help the children more with their homework, but it is the time and the interest that are really important.

She went on to say that she wishes there were more after-school activities for her children so that they could stay involved rather than wandering the street. She said that she knows of some programs, but they are too expensive for her. In reality, there are many after-school activities sponsored by the school that cost nothing. She is apparently unaware of these activities, even though they are important to the academic success of students.

Eloise indicated an interest in sports and in playing the violin during the first visit to the Cejas' home. So, the interest in extracurricular activities is there, but apparently there is nothing being done with that interest. As is to be expected, during the first visit to the house, the Cejas asked a lot of questions about college. Both parents participated in this discussion, which was not really expected given that the father rarely involved himself in the family activities in the poor black homes I studied. During this visit, the two young boys played with their cars in the middle of the living room, while Eloise, Natalie, and Ms. and Mr. Ceja talked to the observers. Mr. Ceja indicated that he would like to help his daughters more but is limited by the language barrier. When one of the observers gave an example of how a university degree can lead to a good job with high pay, Mr. Ceja responded, "Listen, *mija* [my daughter], see, you could do whatever you want." Clearly, the Cejas are interested in, and concerned about, the education of their children, and they express this interest to the children, though the father's comments seemed to be directed at Natalie, who is doing well, and not at Eloise. He said that he constantly tells Natalie to go to college. While he said this, Eloise looked down and away, as though these comments and this concern did not apply to her.

I cannot stress too much how involved Mr. Ceja seems to be in the family life and guidance of the children, or at least of Natalie. This was simply something rarely seen among the black families studied. Whether this is unique to Mr. Ceja or represents a difference between the poor black and the poor Latino families remains to be seen. In the case of the Cejas, though, it would take some of the pressure to prepare the children for the educational experience off Ms. Ceja and stress even more the importance of education to the children.

Ms. Ceja told the two boys to pick up their mess if they were finished playing with their cars, adding that if they did not clean up after themselves, she would not allow them to play the next time. When Dennis, the three-year-old, began to get a bit loud, she told him to quiet down, and he did so right away. It appears that she demands both responsibility and discipline, both qualities necessary in the educational experience.

While the Ceja home is small and sparsely furnished, there are four computers in the house. Dennis sleeps in the room with his parents, the two girls share a room, and Devin sleeps in a room that seems to have been a closet at one time. When the observer went with Eloise and Natalie to their room, Natalie indicated that she plays the clarinet, apparently in the school band, and Eloise said that she plays the violin but not in the band. When they all went back to the living room so that the girls could play a song on the piano for the observers, the parents applauded them, and Mr. Ceja again asked about college, taking the lead in the discussion.

During the next visit Natalie said that normally, after dinner and homework, the children either watch television or play outside. This week, however, Eloise could not watch the television because she was being punished for being involved in fights almost every day at school. Eloise explained that there are different groups at her school, and that when one member of a group is alone, members of the other groups might start a fight. Natalie then pointed out that she was not a member of such a group. Eloise told her that that was because she was only in the sixth grade and that when she got to the seventh grade membership would be necessary. "That's what you said last year," replied Natalie. "Next year you are going to need to be in a group. People are going to mess with you," answered Eloise. "I don't think so. I don't look for trouble. You go around looking for trouble," Natalie responded.

Eloise explained that there were three members of her group until her friend died recently. An argument then occurred between the sisters over whether the friend had "died" or had committed suicide, with Natalie insisting that it was suicide and Eloise denying this. This argument grew loud and the observer "thought that for a while they were going to start fighting." Then Dennis, the three-year-old, came into the girls' room to tell them that it was time for dinner. Before dinner, though, there was a discussion about animals during which Eloise announced that she so loved animals that she wants to become a veterinarian. This from the same young lady who admits that she cares nothing about school, gets low grades in every class, and expects only to complete the ninth grade. She seems quite unrealistic.

Dinner was basically grilled hot dogs. Ms. Ceja explained that she did not have time to prepare anything else. Natalie set the table, while Ms. Ceja asked Devin, the seven-year-old, to help her by counting how many hot dogs she was preparing. He counted and replied that there were eight. "And if I want everyone to have two hot dogs, how many do I need in total?" After a pause, he answered, "Sixteen." Ms. Ceja congratulated him and patted him on the back. Of course this kind of activity, which requires the seven-year-old to count and to think and rewards him for both, is good not only because it shows Devin that these things are important to his mother and therefore should be important to him but also because they are good for his self-esteem. The fact that Eloise is not permitted to watch the television because of her fights suggests discipline, which is of course one of the crucial characteristics of a household in which the children perform well in school. Unfortunately, it seems to have little impact upon Eloise.

The dinner plates had the name of Mr. Ceja's workplace on them, and the cups from which they drank their Jarritos, a Mexican-brand soda, were small plastic cups. During dinner, Ms. Ceja admonished Eloise for not eating "right"—that is, for not eating the right foods (too much candy)—and asked who had not completed her homework. Afterward, there was a discussion about which girl should do the dishes that day, with each sister saying that it was the other's turn. Again, Ms. Ceja shows her interest in and concern about the homework, and we also see that the girls do seem to have household chores to do. These chores help to build a sense of responsibility. Natalie said that she had completed hers, and Eloise said that she did not have any homework. Her mother replied that this was always her excuse for doing no homework.

Eloise asked to go to the park to play baseball, but her mother said that she could not until she completed the homework. Instead of doing the schoolwork, both girls went into the yard to play, after Ms. Ceja excused them both from cleaning up the kitchen. In the yard was a place to wash clothes, as is often done in Mexico; the house does not have a washer or dryer. Three-year-old Dennis urinated next to the garage while the children were playing outside. The girls smiled, while Natalie demanded that he pull his underwear up, which he did. After the children had played for a bit, the observers left.

When the observers arrived for the next observation, only Eloise was at home. Natalie had gone to visit a friend, and the other family members were at a hardware store. After noticing that one of the observers yawned occasionally, Eloise asked whether she was tired. When told that she was, Eloise asked why. The observer explained that she had been awake all night doing homework and had been in class all day. Eloise responded, "So don't do it. Why do it? I would rather sleep. Who cares about homework?" Eloise had told the observer that she had been given detention at school and had gone home immediately afterward. In fact, she had detention every day until school was over in about a month.

"Well, I have to do it [the homework] and care if I want to graduate," responded the observer. "So, do we have to go to college after high school?" asked Eloise. "You literally don't have to, you aren't forced to do anything. However, in a sense, you kind of do if you ever want to make anything of yourself," the observer answered. "Do you have to finish high school?" asked Eloise. "Well, technically students are only required to be in school until they are sixteen." "Good! I am not going to college. And after I am sixteen, I won't have to go to school at all," Eloise said.

After a bit, Mr. and Ms. Ceja and the boys arrived, and Mr. Ceja and the boys went into the basement to watch television. When Natalie arrived a few minutes later, her mother asked about her day and said that she had gone to the lake with her friend. Ms. Ceja said that she had wanted to take Natalie to the lake that day. In fact, she repeated this several times. Eloise was not invited. In fact, Ms. Ceja made no eye contact with Eloise at all during this conversation.

Mr. Ceja joined them soon afterward, and the conversation shifted to how life is easier in Mexico because there are fewer things to worry about and, while poor, people can live happy lives. As Ms. Ceja told stories about their life in Mexico, Natalie was active in the conversation, while Eloise was interested only when there was talk of stealing candy. There was no mention of homework, no evidence that they did any, no talk about the school day, no indication that any chores were done, no indication of participation in extracurricular activities on the part of either of the girls. While the parents seem to stress education, the kinds of activities that seem to correlate with higher achievement—actions that boost self-esteem, household chores to promote responsibility, activities that encourage internal control and a future orientation—do not appear to be consistently present. They stress education but do not seem consistently to translate this stress into the appropriate activities, and they leave Eloise out of even these sporadic efforts.

During another visit, while the girls and one of the observers talked on the couch, Ms. Ceja and Devin went to the kitchen because it was time for his "lesson." Ms. Ceja said that he was having a difficult time with addition and subtraction, so she was going to try to help him. Working on a large notepad, she went over addition and subtraction problems with him, again showing her concern for how well one of the children is doing in school. On the other hand, when asked about their homework, both of the girls indicated that they had none. In fact, the Ceja girls were not seen doing homework during any of our visits.

On several occasions during the observations, Ms. Ceja disciplined Devin for misbehaving, and she also told him once that he could not watch television until he had completed his homework, again concentrating on numbers. On occasion she worked with him on both the numbers and other homework, concentrating on addition and subtraction.

During the final visit, Eloise and Natalie explained that this was the last day of school for the academic year. Eloise was very happy because she "hates school" and did not want to be there anymore. Natalie, when asked how she had done, replied, "I guess I did OK. I'm in honors right now, but I wanted to be in high honors." Eloise laughed and said, "Bad, of course. You want to see my report card?" The report card showed two D's, two D+'s, and one B+, which she received in Spanish. She had been enrolled in a French class but was "kicked out." She then enrolled in the Spanish class. As they discussed the grades, Devin hit the piano with a stick. Actually, it was not uncommon for him to make quite a bit of noise or to be asked by Natalie to stop the noise. It was always Natalie who paid attention to him and verbally disciplined him.

Ms. Ceja indicated that she really did not quite know what to do about Devin. The teachers have told the parents that he had difficulty being still or quiet in school. When Ms. Ceja was told of this almost daily, she would punish Devin for not behaving properly. But, she pointed out, this "wounded" his self-esteem, giving him no support either at home or at school. She then went to the school and told the teacher to stop giving him the negative faces on his daily papers that signified bad behavior. As Ms. Ceja told the story about how Devin was not allowed to sing in an assembly that was very important to him because he had gotten into a fight with another boy, she began to cry and to talk about how such slights hurt her and her children.

She talked about how Eloise needs a positive role model, someone like the observer, who could show her that there are Latinos "who are doing well and will be successful. There is only so much that I can tell her." Clearly, this is a mother who cares very much about her children and their education. She disciplines them when she feels that it is necessary, and she inquires about school. She works with Devin on his math and his homework. She did not, during our observations, seem to be reading to, or playing with, three-year-old Dennis in a way designed to help him with his cognitive processes, language ability, or thinking ability, though she clearly dealt with him in terms of his ability to distinguish between right and wrong. All of these are things thought to be important parts of preparing a preschooler for the educational process. She is, however, home with Dennis all day, and the observers were present only in the evenings because we wanted to be there when the older children were home. So, it is possible that these activities took place when we were not present.

In terms of values, attitudes, and beliefs, the Cejas appear to be middle-class-but-poor folks. The discipline is not as strict as in the families in which the poor black students did well (Sampson 2002) or as strict as Furstenberg and his colleagues (1999) found to be the case for successful poor children. Ms. Ceja is concerned about the self-esteem of her children, stresses nonaggressive behavior and high educational aspirations, maintains an orderly and structured home environment, all of which seem to contribute to achievement, and expects the children to be responsible. On the other hand, she was not much involved in their schoolwork, but neither were the older girls, and while both she and her husband mentioned working toward a better future for the children, only Natalie seems concerned with that future.

In fact, while the Cejas are worried about Eloise, they pay little attention to her. It is almost as though they believe that there is no hope for her to do well. She feels this as well, because she noted during her interview that she sometimes felt as though her parents were an obstacle to her success. They take note of and encourage Natalie, who does well in school, helps to take care of Devin and Dennis, and causes no problems for her parents. Mr. Ceja was more involved with the family, at least in terms of conversation, than were all but one of the poor black fathers studied. He was not, however, involved in any of the educational activities. He did not ask about schoolwork or attempt to help with that work, though, again, the older girls were not seen doing any homework.

He did not work with Devin on his numbers or his homework. When he was at home, for the most part he watched television in his bedroom. So his words say one thing, but his actions seem to say something else.

The child who does well gets the positive attention, and the preschooler does not seem to benefit from the kind of activities that might help him in school, such as reading and dealing with shapes and colors. Both he and his brother were seen pouting when they did not get their way. This does not promote delayed gratification, which is essential for school success. In fact, no one seemed to pay much attention to their pouting, but neither did it get them what they wanted. In a number of ways, then, there are mixed signals here. The family does some of the things necessary to send a child to school prepared to learn, at least for one of the girls, but fails to do several other important things. Language may be one issue here, since the parents are not fluent in English and therefore could not help the girls too much with schoolwork, were they to do much of it.

But it is not a language difference that has Eloise picking locks or hotwiring cars, getting very poor grades, and getting suspended from school. The language difference does not cause the seven-year-old to do poorly in his math. But Ms. Ceja does work with him on this. She is appalled at the lack of respect that she sees from some children here toward adults, and she points out that this is different from Mexico. At one point she said, "You know, in some ways that is the problem with our [Mexican] culture. We are taught to respect our elders and teachers so much that even when we know something is wrong, we hesitate to stand up for ourselves. And this is the way Natalie is."

That is not the way Eloise is, and this causes her parents some consternation, despite the fact that they want children who stand up for themselves. Ms. Ceja said of Natalie, "Natalie is not as outspoken as Eloise. She doesn't speak up for herself. And I constantly wonder about how beneficial or detrimental this is. In a way it is good, because she is disciplined and doesn't cause trouble, but then it could be bad. If someone is taking advantage of her, she won't say or care much." The language difference is a problem for the Cejas, and the cultural difference may well be a problem for the older girls as well. The parents have attitudes and beliefs, according to Ms. Ceja, that reflect their upbringing in Mexico but that seem to be at odds, to some degree, with what the girls must deal with in Evanston. They must balance the two sets. Natalie seems to do this well, but neither Eloise nor Devin does. Overall, the Cejas seem to do a number of the things that they must in order to send their children to school prepared to learn. Some problems might be attributed to the parental backgrounds, but others cannot.

The atmosphere of the household characterized by order, structure, and quiet, which both Clark (1983) and Sampson (2002) have found seems to promote school success, was only marginally conducive to learning in the Cejas' case. The two boys made a fair amount of noise almost daily, and while Ms. Ceja wants a schedule that seems very orderly, it is not always kept. Having four children and two parents in a small house does not always make it easy to maintain order, but the house is certainly not out of control, and the three school-age children do have places to study if they elect to do so.

THE GOMEZES

The Gomez family has three children: seven-year-old Jose, three-year-old Ellie, and one-year-old Zelma. Ms. Gomez and her husband have lived in

Evanston for thirteen years. Like Ms. Ceja, Ms. Gomez is a housewife, and her husband works in construction. Mr. Gomez completed the ninth grade, while Ms. Gomez completed high school and one year of secretarial school. When asked how important Jose's education was to her, she responded, "Very much," because she wants her son to have a better life than she and her husband have. She indicated that she tries to help Jose with his homework "up to where I know. I always make sure he does his homework." So, like Ms. Ceja, Ms. Gomez wants the best for education possible for her school-age son, and her efforts to help with his schoolwork may be hampered by her lack of ability to speak English.

Ms. Gomez has only visited Jose's school once, but if her English skills are as limited as they appear to be, she may well feel uncomfortable in his school environment. According to Ms. Gomez, Jose is doing "good" in school, and she "hardly ever gets bad complaints about" him. The only thing that stands in Jose's way in terms of getting a good education is "money, because he can't afford some classes." Unlike Ms. Ceja, Ms. Gomez says that she has had no problem with racial discrimination.

Ms. Gomez had a difficult childhood because she "was left without parents at a young age. Me being one of the oldest had to work in the fields, keep the house up, and go to school. I eventually had to quit school because of this." She believes that discipline is very important, and she wants Jose "to study so that he will be successful in life. This is why I'm very strict with him." She rarely reads a newspaper, but she reads to Ellie, the three-year-old, three times a week, and she requires Jose to read to her so that "he will better his reading skills."

When the observer arrived for the first visit, she noticed that more than one family lived at the Gomez address; Ms. Gomez's brother lives upstairs. The children and Ms. Gomez were playing together in the backyard. This is the kind of joint activity that helps to promote a sense of cooperation, which is helpful in school, and also helps the children learn to respect and feel close to the parent, which helps the parent when it comes to child rearing.

The Gomez family lives on the first floor of what was apparently a single family home that had been divided to accommodate two families. In the entrance is a washer and dryer and a sink. The second room is a kitchen/dining room, with a stove and refrigerator but no oven. There really is no living room. The family has two bedrooms, one for the parents and the two girls, and one for Jose. The house is neat but sparsely furnished, and the observer noticed no books.

The conversations between the observer and the family were in Spanish. Jose, the second grader, knows "some English, but it is very limited," even though he has lived in Evanston his whole life and his mother has been here thirteen years. This would cause him problems in school at an early age unless the instruction is bilingual. Jose wanted to show off his spelling ability to the observer while Ms. Gomez played with the girls on the floor. They played with some cubes, a puzzle, and a tea set. This is the kind of activity that helps young children develop a sense of shapes and colors and, again, that important ability to work with others.

Jose indicated that he goes to the library and that he likes reading books. He said that after school he did his homework, then watched cartoons on the television, and then went out to play with friends until about 7:30 P.M. Mr. Gomez arrived at 7:30 and, after playing with Ellie for a few minutes, sat down to eat dinner. When the observer left an hour later, he was asleep, having had no real interaction with Jose, Zelma, or his wife.

Jose said that he liked both soccer and baseball and wanted to play soccer at school, but it cost too much. While the observer played with Jose outside, Ms. Gomez, showing her concern for him, came to check on them about every twenty minutes. She seems caring but had little interaction with Jose, and there was no mention of school that day by Jose, the mother, or the father.

During the next visit Mr. Gomez ate soon after he arrived home and again went to bed, not really interacting with the family at all. Again, Ms. Gomez played on the floor with Ellie and Zelma, and again they played with cubes of different colors. This time Ms. Gomez asked Ellie about the colors of the cubes, and when Ellie gave the correct answer, Ms. Gomez applauded her. When she got the answer wrong, Ms. Gomez corrected her and asked her to try again. This kind of activity not only is good for learning but also helps to improve Ellie's self-esteem and her ability to handle criticism, both crucial if she is to go to school prepared to learn. Ellie then took out play money and began counting the dollar bills to ten. All of this conversation and play took place in Spanish, which may well not be a good thing when Ellie enters school.

After a break for ice cream, Ms. Gomez and the girls again played with puzzles; this time the puzzles had animals and vegetables. Ellie took all of the pieces of the puzzles out and then replaced them correctly. As she did so, Ms. Gomez asked her to identify them, which she did correctly with both puzzles. Ellie then brought out her tea set, and her mother showed her just how to serve tea to guests. Again, all of the conversation took place in Spanish. Ms. Gomez seems to do a number of the things with preschoolers that help to prepare them to go to school ready to learn: working with different colors and shapes, working with numbers, and building self-esteem. At this point, however, we noticed that she had not read to the two girls, though, as was the case for the Ceja family, this could have taken place earlier in the day since Ms. Gomez does not work outside the home.

Both Ms. Ceja and Ms. Gomez, while their incomes were quite limited, stayed at home with their children. In the case of the poor black families, almost all of the women worked. It is also true, however, that only half of the black women had husbands at home, so they almost had to work.

During the next visit, Mr. Gomez asked the observer a few questions about the research and then excused himself to run errands. Ms. Gomez explained that he had to buy a money order to pay for three books that they had believed were going to be free, only to be sent a bill for twenty-five dollars. She asked the observer to look at the bill to determine whether there was any way that she could cancel the order to save the money. After the observer found the way to cancel, Ms. Gomez explained that she wished that she could read and speak English. There is much to be learned from this small incident.

Clearly, this is a poor family. Like many poor families they apparently do not have a checking account and therefore rely upon money orders to conduct business. Also, the lack of English speaking ability is apparent, and is again a liability for the parents, and hinders their ability to properly prepare their children for school. Even if Ms. Gomez were to read to her children she would have to do so in Spanish, while it is likely that their work at school is in English, seriously limiting the impact of her help. Thirteen years in Evanston have not been enough to allow Ms. Gomez to learn the language. When school systems deal with Latino students they would do well to think about the possibility that the parents may not speak or read English well enough to really help the children.

Participation in extracurricular activities helps students learn discipline, raises their self-esteem, and teaches them to cooperate. However, typically, the parent must sign a form giving the child permission to participate in the activity. If the form is in English and the parent cannot understand the form, unless someone interprets the form and its intent, the parents have little idea what is happening. While a child, particularly an older one, may well be able to interpret the form, this leaves the parents at the mercy of the child where many school-related matters are concerned.

During this same visit, Ellie, who was being toilet trained, went to the rest room by herself and was applauded by her mother, showing again that Ms. Gomez realizes the need to pay attention to the children's self-esteem. For the second time, Ellie asked whether the observer had a baby in her tummy. Ms. Gomez later explained that her aunt who lived upstairs is pregnant.

Jose asked the observer to accompany him to a park located next to his school, which is in the southern part of the city, an area with a relatively large and growing Latino population. As they walked to the park, they met two of Jose's friends, black siblings. At the park a large group of young Latino men played soccer, while a group of black teenagers played basketball. The observer and Jose played soccer, stopping several times to discuss cheating, but never loudly, and they always worked out the disagreements. This ability to work together to solve problems rather than fighting is a skill that will serve Jose well in school.

The observer again noticed that neither parent read to the children, and Jose did no homework, nor was he asked about his schoolwork by either parent. Parents need to constantly discuss school and schoolwork with children to let them know just how important the school experience is to the parent and therefore how important it should be to the child.

As Comer (1993) explains, in child development, characteristics such as frustration tolerance, impulse regulation, and delay of gratification are important "pathways." Five pathways are "critically important" for academic success: "social interaction, psycho emotional, moral, speech and language or linguistic, and intellectual-cognitive" (p. 304). It is primarily the parents who have the ability and the responsibility to help the child to develop. All too often we rely upon the schools to do all of this, while focusing primarily upon intellectual-cognitive development. The schools cannot do all of this, and the parents who send their children to school already moving along these pathways give them an advantage.

Reading to and with children, playing with them, teaching them to wait rather than pout, encouraging activities that require cooperation, all of these activities help this development. We are seeing some of this in the Gomez household, but some things appear to be missing, and language may well be a part of the explanation.

During the next visit, Ellie introduced the observer to her cousin, Millie, who lives upstairs. This time Jose was in his room doing homework. In his room he has a television with a VCR, a PlayStation, and a Nintendo 64, but he also has a number of children's books. He worked on the homework for about half an hour. All of the homework was in Spanish, suggesting that his school is in fact sensitive to the language differences in its population. This does not seem to hinder the development of Jose's English, given that he communicated with his black friends in English.

When his homework was complete, he and the observer played a game and then watched a movie. During this time Ellie played with her cousin, while Ms. Gomez washed clothes and prepared dinner. Mr. Gomez was not at home. Ms. Gomez interacted little with the baby.

The next time, Jose answered the door, and Ms. Gomez asked that the observer excuse the mess in the house, explaining that she had been at the hospital for a checkup and had not had the time to clean the house. On the other occasions the house was clean and reasonably orderly. It may well be that it is less the order than the discipline required to maintain that order that is important to a child's success in school.

While his mother cleaned and prepared dinner, Jose watched television, and Ellie asked the observer to read her a book. She brought a pile of children's books, all in Spanish, and the observer asked her to select one of the books. Ellie selected a book about bugs, and the observer read while Ellie listened attentively, occasionally asking questions about the bugs, on occasion making sure that the observer knew that she could name the insects. All the while, Jose watched cartoons on television. A bit later he and the observer played another game before he, the observer, and Ellie went outside to play as Ms. Gomez prepared dinner. Mr. Gomez had not arrived home when the observer left for the evening.

It certainly is positive that Ellie not only wanted someone to read to her but also took part in the learning process. On the other hand, it was not Mr. or Ms. Gomez who did the reading.

When the observer next arrived, Mr. Gomez answered the door and explained that Ms. Gomez was upstairs with the relatives. Ellie was taking a nap, and Jose was playing with his PlayStation. Again, there was no indication that he had worked on schoolwork, and his father said nothing to him at all. A bit later Ms. Gomez returned, and Jose came from his room to ask whether the observer wanted to watch a movie with him and Ellie, who had just gotten up from her nap. These two children seem to play a great deal, and Jose watches television quite a bit. There is rarely any mention of school by either parent or much effort to have Jose concentrate on school or related activities. Neither is there a concerted or consistent effort on the part of either parent to make certain that Ellie is developing the interaction skills, personal control, and language and thinking skills that are critical to good school performance. There are some hit-or-miss efforts to help her think and cooperate, but nothing consistent or structured.

As Ellie, Jose, and the observer watched *Peter Pan*, Ellie asked a number of questions about the movie. Why could some people in the movie fly and she could not? Why did Captain Hook have a hook rather than a hand? These are the kinds of questions that allow a caregiver to stimulate thought and learning, but they were asked of the observer and not of a parent. Ms. Gomez checked to see that the children were "behaving" about every twenty minutes, telling them that they had better "behave." It certainly is not the case that she pays no attention to them or their behavior.

When the observer next arrived, Ms. Gomez was preparing dinner and Ellie was playing with Zelma. A bit later Jose came from the basement, and his mother asked whether he had washed his shorts and socks before he sat down to watch television. Apparently the seven-year-old is being asked to wash some of his clothes, suggesting that he might have some household responsibilities. We had seen no evidence of this before, and while household chores help children to develop a sense of responsibility and discipline, Jose may be a bit young to have such consistent chores. On the other hand, in at least one of the poor black families that I studied, even a five-year-old had such responsibilities.

Ms. Gomez told the observer that she had Jose wash his clothes recently because he had come home often with his clothes full of mud, and she thought it only fair that he take care of his clothes. This certainly teaches Jose responsibility and is important for the educational experience. After talking to the observer for a while, Ms. Gomez went to make certain that Jose had finished his task, only to return to tell him that the shorts were still dirty and that he had to wash them again. When Jose did not get up immediately, she told him that she would count to three, and if he had not gotten up before three, he would have to go to his room. At the count of two, Jose was on his way to rewash his shorts. Clearly, he has learned to be a disciplined young man.

During the next visit, Jose, Zelma, Ellie, and their cousin played with the observer and one another for two hours in the yard, while Ms. Gomez washed clothes and checked on them periodically. Jose and the observer played on the seesaw for a time while singing songs in English; Jose explained that he preferred songs in English to those in Spanish. Ellie and her cousin, on the other hand, seem to know the most recent Spanish pop hits.

After a time, Ms. Gomez came out with ice cream and cones, but insisted that everyone go inside to wash their hands before she made them ice-cream cones. After eating his cone, Jose went to his friend's house a few doors away to play basketball, only to return shortly to announce that he had lost by one point. The rest of the time during this visit was spent playing outside. In fact, Jose and Ellie seem to spend more time playing than anything else. While play can certainly be an educational experience and good preparation for school, it is not clear that the Gomezes systematically use it for these purposes. Mr. Gomez does not appear to be a factor in the upbringing of the children, and Ms. Gomez, while stressing discipline and respect, does not consistently do many of the things that might prepare the children for school. She does seem concerned about their self-esteem and sometimes does things that might help to develop it. She rarely asks Jose about his schoolwork or his school day and allows him to spend most of his time watching television and playing games.

She rarely reads to the younger children, and education is not really discussed. This is not exactly a formula for educational success. The children, while interested and animated, are not really challenged by their parents, though Ms. Gomez does try to teach them on occasion. They seem to work well with others, and Ms. Gomez appears to be supportive and concerned. Jose is confident enough to venture beyond his immediate surroundings, and Ellie is very inquisitive. Jose does not appear to be involved in any extracurricular activities.

The home environment seems orderly, if not particularly quiet, given that the television is on most of the time. I cannot help but wonder what role language plays here. The parents do not know enough English to feel comfortable helping Jose with schoolwork, and perhaps this keeps them from discussing education with him. While Ms. Gomez thinks that their lack of money will limit what their children can do educationally, other poor parents believe that only the child limits himself or herself. The effort to create an environment in which learning is stressed is missing.

THE GALINDOS

Mr. and Ms. Galindo live in an area of south-central Evanston in which a number of Latino families are located. They and their three children have lived in Evanston, in their current house, for two years. Both Mr. and Ms. Galindo immigrated from Mexico. Nine-year-old Eriberto is in third grade; seven-year-old Danny is in second grade; and five-year-old Ana is in kindergarten. Mr. Galindo's brother also lives with them. Ms. Galindo is twenty-nine years old and works part-time at a local social service agency while the children are in school; she is one of the few mothers in the study working outside of her home. Note, however, that she is at home when the children arrive from school. Her husband is a maintenance man at a local public school.

Mr. Galindo completed the fifth grade, while Ms. Galindo completed two years of high school. When we asked Ms. Galindo about the importance of Eriberto's education to her, she indicated that it was very important because she wanted him to be educated "for a better life"; she said she tries to encourage him to do well in school.

She does this by helping him with his homework, by pointing out to him that school and studying are good, and at times by promising presents in exchange for good grades. Ms. Galindo visits Eriberto's school when there are meetings, fairs, or other events. There is no indication that she visits to talk to the teachers or administrators about his work or progress. She said that she feels strange when she visits school because of the language barrier and asks Mr. Galindo to talk to the children's teachers. (As was the case for the two families discussed previously, the interview was conducted in Spanish.) She indicated that she feels "unwelcome" when she visits the school because "there are mostly Anglos." There is no bilingual staff. Here again we see the language issue having a serious impact upon the educational process. It is likely that Ms. Galindo does not really understand what is going on in terms of the children's education, and she is therefore limited in just what she can do to aid them. When there are group events such as fairs, she can attend because she does not have to talk, and it is likely that other Latino parents are there to help her to feel more at ease than in one-on-one situations.

Ms. Galindo believes that only Eriberto's personal will stands in the way of his getting a good education. She pointed out that only once, "a long time ago," did anyone try to prevent Eriberto from doing well in school. In this case, a child teased Eriberto and at one time pushed him. But "my husband spoke to his mother, and the kid stopped," she reported. It appears more likely that this was just a child being cruel, as often happens, than that the other student wanted Eriberto to do less well in school.

Ms. Galindo believes that race and/or discrimination plays a role in her life "just by the simple fact that I am Hispanic, and because of the language barrier." Apparently she believes that her Hispanic heritage itself and her inability to speak English cause her to be discriminated against. This is a complex and political issue, of course. Some argue that everyone in the United States should speak English, and that those who do not should not receive the same treatment as those who do. Others argue that institutions in the United States should adapt to the reality that a growing number of folks do not speak English and that this failure should cause them no problems. This is an issue that I shall have to address as I look at the findings and their policy implications in more detail. It is not a simple issue, given the politics and the emotions surrounding it.

Speaking about her upbringing, Ms. Galindo said that she was very dedicated to her studies and to soccer and had a lot of friends. She was a curious young lady and very creative. However, owing to a lack of money, she was unable to continue to attend school and was therefore not able to "follow all that intelligence and creativeness."

When asked how she raises Eriberto, she said that she inculcates a respect for God and everybody. Again, we see the importance of respect to a Latino caregiver. She wants him to respect his body and to be good so that others will respect him. She does not talk to him about the "differences between the races. I don't want him to grow up being racist." So, she apparently believes that knowing about any such differences would make it more likely that Eriberto will become racist. While this is actually counterintuitive, it is what she thinks.

She reads a newspaper about every two weeks, and she reads to her children every two weeks as well. This is simply not enough, especially with the two younger children. But because their schoolwork is in English and she reads only Spanish, she is at a serious disadvantage in performing one of the most important tasks of a caregiver for young children. While she can read to them in Spanish, this is unlikely to help them in a school environment in which everything is done in English. Indeed, it may actually hurt them by delaying their comfort with English.

Like Ms. Gomez, Ms. Galindo relies upon her husband when she has a problem. I stress that this was not the case for the poor black women whose families we studied. They relied upon God or friends and occasionally upon family, but almost never upon a husband. Apparently, Latino men play a somewhat different family role than do poor black men.

Eriberto, the nine-year-old third grader, attends the local public school and most likes his music teacher, his friends, and his physical education teacher. (He refers to his teachers as professors.) It is perhaps instructive that he failed to mention any essential subject teacher. He likes music, his friends, and gym. That will not help much in social studies or math. He least likes writing because "my fingers get hurt." He believes that he is doing "well" in school, and school is "very important" to him, because we wants to increase his intelligence and to get good grades. According to Eriberto, no other student has ever tried to stop him from doing well.

He said that he spends about an hour a day on homework, which would be more time than we have seen any other young student in this study devote to homework. Eriberto said he wants to go as far as fourth grade in school and that he expects to pass to the fourth grade with good grades. It appears that he misunderstood the question, for it is unlikely that he expects to only complete the fourth grade. He sees no obstacles in the way of his education, suggesting that he believes that he is in control of his future—internal control.

Eriberto has never read a newspaper. This makes it rather difficult for him to keep up with current affairs, and while he is young, reading is obviously a good habit to form early. He said that his parents are the most important things in his life and that his music teacher is the closest teacher to him because "he has us do fun activities like playing the guitar." He would not want to change anything about his family life, and he would like to be a "Mexican soccer player" if he could be one person in the world, "because I enjoy that sport and [it] is fun." None of the students interviewed thus far has aspirations of being involved with intellectual activities. While it is tempting to argue that this is a reflection of age, remember that we interviewed two middle school students who are certainly old enough to think about being a physician or a famous attorney or a noted scholar. The higher-achieving poor black students tended to give answers suggesting high aspirations and high self-esteem. I am seeing little of that with the poor Latino students. In fact, while I noticed that all of these students tend to be respectful toward others, the kind of confidence and comfort with self that tends to characterize high achievers seems to be missing.

The Galindos live in a small but neat three-bedroom house. When the observer arrived for the first visit, all three of the children were watching television and Ms. Galindo was cleaning the kitchen. After introductions in Spanish, the observer listened as the children explained the *Power Rangers* show to her. In fact, when Eriberto was asked to answer the questions from the student questionnaire, he responded that he would do so, but only during commercials.

Ms. Galindo explained that the three children had a schedule in which they eat dinner after arriving from school, then watch the television, and then do their homework. She handed Eriberto and Danny school folders, but they ignored them and continued to watch television. In fact, there was no evidence of any educational activity during the visit; the children watched the television and discussed the shows the entire time.

Ms. Galindo takes an English class, apparently at Family Focus, as do a number of the mothers we contacted. They are aware that their inability to speak English hampers them in their daily activities and may well limit their children. Yet, Spanish is still spoken in the homes. The next visit had to be rearranged because Ms. Galindo had forgotten that she had an English class that evening.

When the observer arrived for the next visit, the children were eating dinner (bean tacos) and drinking chocolate milk. When they finished, all three went to the living room to watch television, while Ms. Galindo washed the dishes. Ms. Galindo then showed the observer a math quiz that Eriberto had taken and for which he received a grade of 100 percent. Asked whether he enjoyed math, he enthusiastically replied, "I do very much."

Ms. Galindo told the observer several times that Eriberto was a good student. She indicated that he had been in bilingual education for two years. She noted that Danny needs more support from her when it comes to homework because if she does not supervise him until it is complete, he will not finish it. Ana is in kindergarten and, according to Ms. Galindo, rarely has homework, but she believes that Ana is doing fine in school. During the entire visit the television was never turned off, and none of the children did any homework. Ms. Galindo explained that they rarely have homework for the weekend. She said that Fridays are free time for the children, and she does not force them to do schoolwork.

The good students among the poor black students I studied in Evanston seemed to have schoolwork, not necessarily homework, almost every day. Their parents asked them about school and their assignments every day. They discussed what was going on at school just about every day. I am seeing none of this so far with the Latino families. While the mothers indicate an interest in the education of their children, so far I see little of the attention to the details, little of the constant discussion of school with the children by the parents.

Mr. Galindo works the second shift and is not at home when the children arrive from school. This means that the main burden of helping guide and shape the children has to fall upon Ms. Galindo. Apparently that is the pattern in these households even when the father is not at work.

As was the case during the last observation, there was no educational activity on the part of Ms. Galindo or any of the children. During the next visit the three children watched cartoons on television in the living/dining room, while Ms. Galindo watched television, in Spanish, in the kitchen. Eriberto again indicated that he had no homework, and Ms. Galindo made no effort to ensure that this was the case or to engage him in any discussion about his school day. She does in fact work about six hours a day at a local social services agency but is at home close to the time that the children arrive from school. While she did not indicate this work when responding to the questionnaire, this means that she is the first of the three mothers observed so far who works at all outside of the home. Even so, she is at home when the children are there and is in a position to offer quite a bit of support, help, and encouragement, which could help the children in school, but we have not seen this effort so far.

A friend of Ana's came over, and Ana asked to go outside to play. When Ms. Galindo replied that this was fine, the girls, followed by the two boys, ran outside, leaving the television on; Ms. Galindo watched them occasionally from a window. After a bit Ana asked for permission to go to the playground, and her mother said that she could. The observer accompanied Ms. Galindo and the children to the playground, while Ms. Galindo discussed her unsuccessful efforts to have the children attend the laboratory school across the street from their home. She wanted them there because it is close, it is a good school, and because it is a K– 8 school, so they would not have to leave school after the fifth grade to go to middle school. It seems that logistics and convenience were most important, but at least she indicated concern.

As the children played, they were joined by a young black girl. They spoke Spanish the entire time, however; Ms. Galindo explained that they speak Spanish at home and only speak English in school. A neighbor arrived and invited the Galindo children to her house. At the same time, Mr. Galindo arrived on a half-hour break from his job. The two agreed to let the children go to the neighbor's home, and the observer left, noting again the absence of educational activity and any interaction between Ms. Galindo and the children that might prepare them for school. Their playing with other children helps them to learn to cooperate, but we have little to suggest that Ms. Galindo emphasizes discipline, internal control, delayed gratification, a future orientation, or high educational aspirations. She certainly doesn't ignore the children, but she has thus far shown little inclination or ability to do the kinds of things necessary.

When she arrived for the next visit, the observer found the children again watching television. When asked whether he had any schoolwork, Eriberto replied that both he and Danny had homework, but he said, "I don't know, later," when asked when he planned to do the work. Ms. Galindo's brother-in-law came out of the shower, greeted the observer in Spanish, and went into his room to watch television. After a time Ms. Galindo came from her room to give Eriberto a one-page math assignment and Danny a five-page spelling homework assignment, while Ana continued to watch television. The boys went to the small dining-room table to work, with the television still on. In fact, they both watched the television and focused on the schoolwork only during the commercials.

Fifteen minutes later Ms. Galindo informed the observer that there was a presentation at Family Focus that she and the children were to attend. When the children heard her mention the presentation, they yelled in Spanish, "Yes, let's go, Mom." So, after fifteen minutes of homework, during which they watched television and received no encouragement from their mother, they left for Family Focus.

Once at Family Focus, the Galindo family, including the uncle, and the observer shared a dinner table with a black family, and Ana immediately began to talk with the young girl seated next to her. The presentation was about different live animals, and during the presentation Eriberto was the child who responded to most of the questions raised by the animal owners/handlers, suggesting both his comfort level in groups and his curiosity and intelligence. All three of the Galindo children interacted well with the other children, including those of different ages and races.

During the next visit, the children played in the backyard before asking permission to go to the park on their bicycles. Ms. Galindo agreed and told the observer that the children were not allowed on the streets without adult supervision. So, as is the case for the two other mothers observed so far, Ms. Galindo watches over the children quite a bit. While Eriberto told the observer, in response to her question, that he had homework, he had done none of it during the almost two hours that the children played either in the backyard or the playground.

The next two visits took place after school was out for the summer, so the children were at home during the day. Each child told the observer that they had passed to the next grade and that they had received good grades, though in the Evanston elementary grades the students do not receive letter grades. After a time, Mr. Galindo arrived (apparently, since the school at which he works was out, his hours had changed). He sat with the children and the observer outside of the house for a time before going to the grocery store with Ana.

After eating dinner, the children and the observer went to watch television in the living room, while Mr. and Ms. Galindo cleaned the kitchen. When the children heard the bells of the ice-cream truck outside, Ana asked her father for money to buy ice cream, only to be told that they did not have the money. She began to cry, but her parents did not change their minds, rather offering her ice cream from their freezer. She finally stopped crying and accepted the ice cream offered. So, the parents do expect some discipline. The children had gotten a young rabbit as a pet. When they played with the rabbit outside, Mr. Galindo sat with them but showed no interest and did not say anything that might have helped the children classify or generalize, activities that can mean a great deal in the learning process.

After Ana's friend arrived a few minutes later, Ms. Galindo decided to take the children to the park for a bike ride. As the observer left, Mr. Galindo mentioned to her that he wanted to remain in Evanston because Northwestern University and other universities were located in or near the area, which provided an opportunity for his children. Clearly, he is not only thinking about their college education but perhaps expecting them to attend college, despite the fact that the family is poor.

One of the characteristics of the homes of high-achieving poor students identified by Clark (1983) is that the parents expect the child to receive postsecondary training. This is only the second time we have heard this or seen any evidence of this from the three families studied so far. Clark also identified a number of other characteristics of the families of high-achieving students of which I have seen little, including frequent school contact initiated by the parents; achievement-centered parental rules and norms; frequent parental involvement in achievement-training activities.

Entwisle, Alexander, and Olson (1997) studied students about to enter the first grade, and Clark studied high-school-aged students, so the work of Entwisle and Alexander may be more relevant to this work. They identify a number of family and student characteristics thought to be associated with higher student achievement. Students who do well in school are enthusiastic and cheerful, as opposed to timid and reclusive; they are polite and considerate, as opposed to bellicose and combative; they concentrate well; they are cooperative and helpful; they learn quickly; they help with household chores; they have parents who understand and listen to them and who care about their feelings; they have parents who feel that what they do is important.

Both Entwisle and Alexander and Clark stress discipline; internal control; high educational aspirations; responsibility; a quiet, orderly home environment; and a positive self-image. It is the responsibility of the parents, the primary caregivers, to provide both the actions and the environment that foster these characteristics.

Thus far I have seen little evidence that the Latino parents do the necessary things. However, there is little conflict in the homes; the students are calm with the parents; the parents do in fact monitor the children's activities frequently; and the children studied thus far do seem to accept the parental norms, with the exception of Eloise Ceja. All of these are also characteristics of the homes in which students perform well. The characteristics related more directly to learning and school are the ones that seem to be most lacking. Those related to comportment are more in evidence. The language barrier may be at work in that it limits the interaction with, and understanding of, school and perhaps learning-related activities. The comportment-related activities may well be connected with the emphasis on respect in the Latino household. The children are, for the most part, calm, respectful, helpful, and cheerful, so they may be in a position to absorb the lessons and develop the characteristics more directly related to education; but the necessary educational emphasis and related activities seem to be in short supply.

The last visit to the Galindo home also occurred during the summer break, a time when activities such as organized sports, going to the library, and taking various lessons (music, dance, sports) may take place and are known to be helpful to students. While the lack of money may limit some of these activities for poor families, it does not eliminate them all, since many are free or subsidized for those with limited funds.

During this visit the children were initially playing in the backyard; then they went into the house to watch an animated movie. When asked whether he preferred to be in school or on break, Eriberto excitedly answered that he enjoys the summer because he dislikes reading—not a good sign. As usual, the children were well mannered and cheerful, but also as usual, all they did was play and watch television. They are well behaved, but they are not being particularly well prepared for the educational experience, perhaps because of language, and perhaps because poor Latino families respect teachers and administrators so much that they expect them to do most of the educational work. In any event, so far I have not seen much preparation.

THE RANGELS

The Rangels, who came to Evanston from Mexico, have one child, three-year-old Mary, and Ms. Rangel was pregnant at the time of the study. She and her husband have lived in Evanston for nine years and in the same house for six years. Mr. Rangel's brother, his wife, and their two children also live in the basement of the house. Mr. Rangel is employed in the home-remodeling business, and Ms. Rangel is a housewife. Mr. Rangel attended *la prepa*, roughly equivalent to college in the United States; it is not clear whether he graduated. But because he cannot speak English, "he can only work remodeling houses."

Ms. Rangel attended high school in Mexico but received her GED, with her "husband's support," in the United States. When asked how important Mary's education was to her, she replied "very important," because it is important to be "conditioned from a young age to be better academically in the future." She said that she encourages Mary to do well academically by urging her to try again when she becomes frustrated with her preschool work. She visits the preschool three times a week and spends an entire day there once a month, feeling comfortable each time. Her upbringing was difficult in part because she had no relationship with her father. She never reads a newspaper but reads a book every day.

As the observer completed the questionnaire with Ms. Rangel, Mary came running into the living room and wanted to play hide-and-seek with the observer. After the observer "found" her in her parent's bedroom hiding under her baby bed, she showed the observer her playroom, which had numerous pieces of "art" that Mary had drawn in her preschool. She then ran to hide in the backyard and the basement, where her aunt and uncle live.

In three of the four families observed so far, other relatives also live in the house. This of course reduces living expenses, but it could also give the family another source of emotional and educational support. Thus far, I have not seen any of the relatives play either of these roles.

Ms. Rangel finally came to the basement and told Mary that the observer was going to leave if Mary did not play with her, so Mary went to the back-yard to play. Ms. Rangel was teaching Mary that she has to cooperate to get what she wants, a very valuable lesson indeed. Ms. Rangel brought the ob-server, Mary, and Mary's friend Lia some fruit and juice, serving the fruit on paper plates. After more playing, Ms. Rangel informed everyone that snacks were ready, again served on paper plates, this time in the kitchen.

Mary began to cry, for no apparent reason. It turns out, however, that Lia was sitting in the seat used by Mr. Rangel, and this bothered Mary because she wanted to sit there. Ms. Rangel asked Lia to move, thus accommodating Mary and perhaps missing an opportunity to teach Mary to share or to be pa-tient. For the remainder of the visit Mary played either indoors or outdoors. She played more hide-and-seek, rode her tricycle, and asked to go to the cor-ner with the observer. She is an active young lady.

The Rangels, like most of the Latino families, live in a diverse neighbor-hood in Evanston, in a formerly largely black area seeing significant growth in the Latino population. Their house is small but neat, and the living room has one bookshelf cluttered with movies and books in both Spanish and English. Mary speaks primarily Spanish. Her preschool classes, which she attends on Monday, Wednesday, and Friday, are conducted in Spanish. In fact, Ms. Rangel indicated that she thought it important that Mary know Spanish first and then English. However, Mary spoke to her friend Lia in English, using only short phrases, but enough to suggest that she does know the language. The fact that the primary language of the house is Spanish may put Mary at some disadvantage when she enters school and may, as I have in-dicated earlier, put her in the position of go-between for her parents and the school.

Mary takes swimming classes during the week. She is not allowed to watch television until late in the day, and then, according to her mother, she watches only educational programs. While she played with the observer and Lia, at one point she called out random numbers. She always said "please" and "thank you" when her mother served her food or snacks. When Mary was outside, Ms. Rangel, as did the other Latino mothers, looked out to check on her every ten minutes or so. Ms. Rangel made certain that Mary included both the observer and Lia in her play activities. At one point she wanted to watch a movie, but her mother asked her to wait, which she did without rancor, suggesting that she is being taught to delay gratification. So, she seems to work (play) well with others, is well behaved and energetic, and is learning to delay gratification, all characteristics that should serve her well in school.

Once during this first observation Mary asked her mother to read to her, but Ms. Rangel had just begun to cook. The observer volunteered to read, and Mary energetically brought her a book in Spanish, to which she responded "excitedly" and whose plot she already knew. When that book was finished, she brought three more to read. Clearly, someone, probably Ms. Rangel, reads to her often. This is the first evidence I have seen of a preschooler being read to and responding to that reading.

During the next visit, after Mary awoke from a nap, she began to roll on the floor in the bedroom that she shares with her parents. When Ms. Rangel told her to get up and go to the living room with the observer to play and to tell her about her preschool activities that day, Mary responded that she did not want to go unless she talked to her father on the phone. Ms. Rangel called him, and after some discussion with Mary, he hung up and Mary went to play with the observer. She seems to get much of what she wants from her parents much of the time.

At one point Ms. Rangel had to tell Mary that the observer would leave if Mary did not pay some attention to her. Ms. Rangel has said this several times now, suggesting that she may be trying to teach Mary to be cooperative. Mary asked her mother to read to her, and Ms. Rangel asked the observer to read since she was again cooking. This time one of the books that Mary brought was in English, and Mary told her mother that she had the wrong book. Ms. Rangel informed the observer that Mary already knew the book and that she and her husband would translate the books into Spanish for Mary. Again, she is encouraged to speak, read, and learn Spanish at home rather than English, which will certainly not help her in a non-bilingual educational setting. On the other hand, she is being read to and apparently enjoys the activity. She also knows many colors, though we have yet to see her parents engage her in any activity that might be educational. Since she knows several of the books the observer read to her, I assume that someone in the home is reading to her. However, she is in preschool classes, and it is likely that she encounters reading and the identification of colors there.

After Ms. Rangel informed the observer that Mary was very attached to Mr. Rangel but that he was not very involved in her life because he worked so much, mother and daughter went to Family Focus for a carnival, accompanied by Mary's cousin Jesus, who lives downstairs. When they returned home, Mr. Rangel greeted them, and Ms. Rangel said that Mary usually runs to him and asks him to read to her as soon as he gets home. They hugged, and after Ms. Rangel introduced the observer to her husband, the observation ended.

Ms. Rangel delivered her baby, a boy, three months early. While this caused some problems with the observations, they did in fact continue. During one of the observations Mary showed the observer her coloring book, showing all of the pages that she had colored with her father. When Ms. Rangel turned on the radio in the kitchen, Mary asked her to turn it off. Her mother responded that Mary should not act silly and that the observer would leave if Mary continued to act that way, a threat repeated often during the observations. Mary asked to play some music tapes, and when her mother told her not to do so, she had a tantrum. When her mother told her that she would tell her father that she was not behaving well, she ran to her room, only to return a few minutes later, clearly angry.

While playing with her coloring book with the observer, she again became angry and snatched the book. Her mother again told her that if she did not act nicely the observer would leave, but no matter what, she remained upset. Her mother apologized, explaining that she had not had her nap and was perhaps cranky because of that. No matter what the observer said or did, Mary would not look at her. When her father arrived, she ran to him and told him that she wanted to color in the book. They went to the bedroom and did not return during the visit.

This young lady appears to have her way quite often, despite the efforts of her mother. She seems very close to her father, but neither parent seems to engage her much in educational or stimulating activity. They do not encourage or motivate her. While she seems very close to her father, it is not clear that he uses this relationship to teach her the characteristics that she will need to do well in school, despite what seems to be her inquisitive nature. The lessons from her mother to delay gratification are infrequent and inconsistent, as evidenced by her tendency to pout when she does not get her way. While this may well be common for a young child who is the only child, it will not serve her well as she enters school, which requires the ability to delay gratification.

The next visit was cut short because Ms. Rangel had to go to the hospital after a call regarding her newborn son, but during the visit Mary told the observer that her brother would be coming home soon. When asked who told her that the baby was coming home soon, she said that no one had told her but she knew since her father was almost through painting the room into which she would move. If the room was close to complete, the baby must be arriving soon. An interesting piece of deduction.

During the next visit Mary played in the backyard with her two cousins from downstairs in a small plastic wading pool. When her mother asked her to get out of the pool, she refused and continued to play. The observer spent the entire visit playing with and watching the children play in the yard. After a time the aunt arrived, but neither she nor Ms. Rangel used the opportunity to teach, nurture, or motivate the children, who played with leaves from the yard, pretended to make a piñata, and sang a song with the observer. It would seem that there have been a number of opportunities for Ms. Rangel to teach Mary or to show interest in what excites her or catches her attention, but these opportunities for the most part go unused.

According to Edwards (1995), children Mary's age, and therefore their parents, face six unique and important developmental tasks: learning how to function independently or interdependently; developing self-concept and self-reflection; developing impulse- and self-control; beginning to develop a sense of morality; establishing gender identity; and becoming a member of the larger society. Cultures and parents may differ in the importance attached to each of these tasks and in the age at which they expect the tasks to be mastered. Still, if the child is to develop well along the pathways laid out by Comer (1993), he or she will master them, and the parent or primary caregiver is essential to this development (Laosa and Sigel 1982).

This development is essential in preparing the child for school, and I did not see Ms. Rangel play much of a role in this process. Mary is a precocious three-year-old who appears to want to be challenged and to show off what she has learned. It seems, however, that her mother may assign to the preschool that Mary attends the tasks of her development, when that is in fact her role. Mr. Rangel plays very little part in Mary's development. This is not unusual in the Latino families observed thus far. While the father is present in the home in all of those families, it appears that his main role is to work to supply the money. The mothers generally stay at home and take care of the father, the house, and the children. This gives the mothers a great opportunity to help the children to develop and to prepare them for school, but I do not see that they are doing this systematically or consistently.

THE PEREZES

Mr. and Ms. Perez and their two children, Alex, aged ten, and Annette, aged seven, live in a small house in the north-central part of Evanston. The neighborhood has for many years been the heart of the black community, but over the past five years it has seen more and more Latino residents, to the consternation of many of the black inhabitants. The area is changing so much and so rapidly that the local branch of Family Focus, which has been a staple of the community for years as it served the poor blacks, has now begun to reach out to the growing Latino population, hiring its first Latino staffer.

The Perezes have lived in Evanston, and in their house, for six years; both are from Mexico. Ms. Perez works in child care, and it is unclear just what Mr. Perez does. Mr. Perez completed the sixth grade, while Ms. Perez completed the seventh grade in Mexico but received her GED in the United States. When asked how important Alex's education is to her, she responded, "Very important. We always try to keep him interested in studying, doing well in school, as motivation to have a better future and a better life." The observer failed to ask about the importance of Annette's education. This was a mistake. Given Annette's young age, we did not administer the questionnaire to her. However, as was the case for all of the twenty-one children involved in the research, we did observe her in the home setting. Like all of the other mothers studied thus far, Ms. Perez answered the questions in Spanish, and like the others, she believes that the education of her son is very important. Unlike the others, Ms. Perez mentioned specific actions taken to help prepare Alex for his education.

She indicated that she helps Alex do his research for homework, and she tries "to keep myself informed with what happens inside the school," visiting the school "when there are events held at school." She said that she feels "happy and confident" when she visits, unlike most of the others interviewed thus far. She says that she is treated "well; there is staff that helps translate when needed and because it makes Alex feel important when parents visit the school." Obviously, she understands the impact on Alex's self-esteem of parental visits to school, but she appears to have the same language problems as the other parents. Somehow Ms. Perez does not allow this barrier to intimidate her. She indicated, however, that she visits the school when events are held. Parents who are closely involved with the education of their children, particularly younger children, tend to visit the school more often and have more intimate meetings with staff.

Alex is bused from his neighborhood to a school in a more affluent area of Evanston for integration purposes. Years ago, the only elementary school in the black community was closed so that most black students would have to be bused out to integrate schools that were almost all white. As Latinos move into the neighborhood, some of them, like Alex, are being bused out as well. According to Ms. Perez, the only thing that stands in the way of Alex's receiving a good education is some of his classmates on his school bus. Some of them, she said, try to stop Alex from doing well in school by calling him names and using "bad words." "Once he didn't want to go to school because one of his classmates was bugging him and he did not want his mom to intervene." This really sounds more like young boys being young boys than an effort by other students to hold back his academic progress. Actually, I have seen almost no evidence of this type of effort on the part of other students. However, the families in this study had only two children of middle-school age. The type of antiachievement pressure noted by Fordham and Ogbu (1986) is most likely at or above the middle-school age, particularly since letter grades are not given in Evanston until middle school.

Like most of the other women interviewed so far, Ms. Perez said that her upbringing was "not good economically. Going to school was difficult because I also had to help with household chores, help my mother out, and being the youngest in the family, [I] got tired of going to school and started working at the age of twelve." While poverty is certainly difficult for many Americans, the idea of having to work at age twelve to help the family is foreign to most people raised in this country, even those poor blacks whom I studied in Evanston. While this experience may well provide a powerful incentive to the parents to ensure that their children receive a good education, it also limits their ability to do so. Their financial resources are limited, as well as the kind of life experiences that may help their children. Still, many poor nonwhites do well in school and rise from poverty. They, however, have families who provide the necessary framework, home environment, and values to allow this to happen. So far it is not clear that the Latino families studied do this, at least not consistently.

When asked how she and her husband try to raise Alex, Ms. Perez responded, "I try to implement respect, not to lie, and if (he) continues to go to school, he will have a better future and be economically stable as well as the unity within the family." Here again, we see the importance of respect and family to Latinos. Over 91 percent of the respondents to Grossman's (1995) questionnaire agreed with the statement "The family is the most valued institution in the Hispanic culture." While this may well put the family in a position to greatly influence the degree to which the student is prepared for school, it also may limit the student if the family fails to do the things that enhance the probability of academic success. The respect that is so important to Latino families may help a child where discipline is concerned but down the road may limit the child's inclination to challenge, to explore, or to disagree, especially with elders.

Like the others interviewed, Ms. Perez "rarely" reads a newspaper, so she cannot really talk to Alex about the issues of the day or encourage him to read or think about them. Also like most of the others, she relies upon her spouse when she has a problem, still another indication of the importance of the families in Latino culture. But the fact that Mr. Perez doesn't really speak English would seem to limit the amount of help that he can offer where the children and school are concerned.

Ms. Perez has learned English, and Mr. Perez is going to school as well, according to Ms. Perez. She seems to understand how much the language barrier can cost her children, and she wants to do something about it. The other mothers studied thus far either do not see the importance of the issue or believe that Spanish should be the language of the house, despite the limits that this may impose upon both the parents and the children as far as their education is concerned.

Ms. Perez also said that she and her husband try to keep Alex busy by having him join the school band and urging him to play baseball. Involvement in extracurricular activities such as these help the student to develop discipline, higher self-esteem, and the ability to cooperate.

Ten-year-old Alex is in the fourth grade and most likes reducing fractions, math, and reading. He least likes it when he and his friends are playing and they throw the ball "too far away." He says that he is doing "very well" in school and that school is very important to him because "we can learn a lot of things, things that our teachers teach us." According to Alex, no student has ever tried to stop him from doing well in school, which supports my assumption that the activity on his school bus is aimed less at limiting his academic achievement than finding something with which to bother another student, an activity prized by many young boys.

Alex says that he devotes a half hour to an hour every evening to his homework and expects to go "all the way, to college." The obstacle that he sees is that on the school bus "kids call each other names. Some misbehave and we usually get in trouble for what the others say or do." If Grossman (1995) is correct when he suggests that cooperation is a part of the Latino culture, then this name-calling and apparently aggressive behavior on the part of some students on the bus would bother Alex and his mother more than perhaps it should. Most of the students being bused to the school attended by Alex are poor black students for many of whom aggression is a way of life, and often little is meant by it. Furthermore, his success would not threaten the poor black students in his neighborhood or in his school since they are unlikely to view him as part of their group.

Alex reads the newspaper only if he needs to do so as part of a homework assignment. He says that learning is the most important thing in his life, an answer not offered by the other students interviewed thus far. Alex indicated that his father helps him with his homework when he finds the work too difficult. Having the father help with homework at all is unusual for both the poor blacks and the poor Latinos studied. Helping with schoolwork, when it is done by a parent at all, is usually done by the mother, even when the father is present in the home. This help is offered consistently in the homes in which children do well in school and not at all in the homes in which they perform poorly.

Having Mr. Perez help with the work presents an interesting issue. He is apparently not fluent in English, so his ability to help with a number of subjects would be limited. On the other hand, the actual help is less important than the message about the value of the work to the parent.

When asked whom he would choose to be like if he could be like any one person in the world, Alex responded, "My parents, because they are parents." Again, we see the two dominant themes in the Latino household: the importance of the family and respect for elders.

Like the homes of the other Latino families studied, the Perez home is quite small but very neat and well kept. The living room is divided into a living area and a small study area with a number of books, a computer, and an encyclopedia set. Ms. Perez watches over two other small children, a boy and a girl who seem to be about the same ages as Annette and Alex, who live in the basement, until their mother comes home from work. The children arrive home from school between 4 and 4:30 P.M.

On the day of the first observation Alex set up his game of Nintendo to play with the others, but after setting it up, he pulled out his book bag and took out his homework. At that point Ms. Perez asked the other children whether they had any homework, though she seemed to focus on Annette. The children she cares for said that they had no homework, and she remarked that they never seem to have any homework.

Alex began his homework while the others played Nintendo. He looked up at them every now and then and asked whether they needed any help and then went back to his work. Annette, who did have homework, worked on it but was distracted by the game being played by the other two children. Alex asked his sister how much homework she had. When she replied that she had one sheet, he told her that they were lucky not to have so much homework but that he couldn't wait to get to high school, even though he knows that he will have a lot of homework every day. He then returned to his homework. Alex appears to be a conscientious and disciplined student. He began his homework with no prompting, suggesting that this is routine for him, and even asked his sister about her work. While the children from downstairs played, he worked.

A bit later Mr. Perez arrived from work and, after asking his children about their homework, took out one of the books from the encyclopedia set and began to read. Alex continued his homework, while Annette waited her turn in the game. Mr. Perez seemed to notice that the game distracted Alex somewhat and asked the children to turn it off, which they did right away.

Whenever Alex encountered a word that he did not understand in English, he would ask his parents to help him translate the word into Spanish, again suggesting how difficult school can be when language is a problem. At least in the Perez household, the mother speaks both languages. Imagine how it must be for the student when neither parent can translate. This lack of language skill may also dampen the urge of the parents to help at all, when the offer to assist is critical.

Ms. Perez had to insist that Annette do her work, and once that was complete she was to read one of the books she takes home every day to read. When she showed no interest in doing her reading, Mr. Perez suggested that she read at least one page, which she reluctantly did. All of this is very different from what we have seen with the other families. Both parents seem involved with the students' schoolwork, sending a powerful message about the importance of that work. Alex seems more concerned with his work than with playing a game. Schoolwork appears to be a part of the day for the children. Annette is being taught to study and learn beyond what is assigned. The parents attempt to limit distractions so that the children have a better work environment. While these are all things routinely done in the homes of middle-class people, even those who are poor (Sampson 2002), they are seldom done in the homes of students who do poorly in school. I have not seen them done often in the homes of the other families studied, despite what the parents say about the importance of education.

Alex spent an hour on his homework and then took a package of instant soup from the pantry. His mother helped him to prepare it, while Mr. Perez talked about how Alex played the flute in the school band and belonged to a Little League baseball team. His parents offered him various options in terms of both instruments and sports, and he seems comfortable, according to his father, with his selections. The overall development of their children is clearly a priority for the Perez parents, and they seem to be willing to do some of the things that will help that growth and development.

When Alex completed his homework, he asked permission to go outside to play with the others, who were already playing. While Ms. Perez watched the children play, she explained that in addition to the children from the basement, she watches the children of the mothers who are taking GED lessons at Family Focus while they are in class. She also told the observer that when they purchased their house six years ago, it was in very bad condition, which made it affordable. Mr. Perez did the fix-up work himself while working at the local hospital and attending English classes at a local community college. This is a motivated man. His wife explained that since he had not been allowed the opportunity to receive much education, it was important to him that his children have that chance. While I have heard other Latino parents, mostly mothers, say much the same thing, I have rarely seen them do the kinds of things being done in the Perez household.

While the children played, the observer and the parents discussed the importance of their decision to move to the United States. The observer's parents had made the same decision for the same reason: to find a better life. In fact, all of the observers were Latino, and most had parents who had recently migrated from Mexico.

When the observer arrived for the next visit, Alex, Annette, and the two children from downstairs were eating dinner. As soon as they finished, Alex said that he was ready to go to band practice. But before he could go, he took out his schoolbag and began to work on his homework, telling his mother that he had only a few worksheets to complete. As he worked, a loud noise came from downstairs, indicating that the father of the other two children was at home. Ms. Perez again asked them whether they had homework, and again they replied that they did not. Alex responded, "Man, you're lucky. I wish I didn't get any homework like you." He then continued his own work.

Annette took out her own schoolwork, which was mostly coloring, and her brother remarked that her work was easy compared to his. He then took out a worksheet that was apparently optional. When he completed this sheet, his father arrived from work, and the parents dropped the observer and the children off at the school while they ran errands. Alex knew right away where to go, took out his flute, and waited for the instructor to tell the band what to do. Alex was one of two Latinos in the band. Since the school is located in one of the more affluent areas of Evanston and is quite a distance from the Perez home, Alex's participation in the band is somewhat of a hardship on the Perez family. Yet, they not only encourage his participation but also make it possible logistically. They seem to understand the value of his participation in extracurricular activities, while the other parents studied so far do not.

During the one-hour band practice Alex was attentive and serious. The Perezes arrived at the end of the hour and drove the children and the observer back to their home. As soon as they arrived, Annette and Alex asked permission to play outside with the children from downstairs. During this time of play, Alex spoke a mixture of Spanish and English, and the children all seemed to understand one another. When Mr. Perez returned from running errands, he again sat down to read one of the volumes of the encyclopedia before joining his wife and the observer in a conversation about Annette's lack of interest in reading. They remind Alex that it is important for him to do well in school, and he responds by doing his schoolwork right away when he arrives home, but Annette constantly offers excuses to avoid reading. While they offer the same support and encouragement to both children, when the young girl protests, she seems to get away with it, while the boy perhaps did not.

A bit later the children were called in to take a shower, but they both protested. This lasted only until Mr. Perez told them that it was time for their shower. The protests then stopped immediately. This level of involvement by the father with child rearing is something that I have not seen previously. It helps not only Ms. Perez but also the children in terms of the development of discipline.

When the observer arrived for the next visit, Alex was doing his spelling homework and Annette was coloring in a book. When Alex needed help translating into English a few words that he wanted to add to his sentences, he asked his mother for help. When he completed the spelling work, he proceeded to his math homework.

After Alex told the observer that his favorite subject was science, he explained to the observer and to his mother what he had recently learned about precipitation. Ms. Perez continually complimented him and mentioned several times that Alex reads many science books, which he takes from the library during his free time, all the while helping to boost his self-esteem.

When the homework was complete, Alex got his baseball glove and shoes and informed his mother that he was ready for baseball practice. The observer, Ms. Perez, and both children then drove to the park where Alex practiced on Wednesdays. While he practiced with the team, Annette and her mother went to the other side of the park so that Annette could play on the swings. As they drove home after practice, Alex excitedly told his mother about what he and his teammates had done that day. When they arrived home, he and his sister asked to go outside to play with the neighbors from downstairs, who were already out. The downstairs children seem to do little but play, while Alex and Annette do schoolwork and clean up their rooms, and Alex is involved in two extracurricular organized activities. The Perez children are learning discipline, internal control, the ability to delay gratification, and the importance of education, while the children from downstairs appear to be learning to play.

At the start of the next visit both Annette and Alex were playing on the play lot close to their house with the children from downstairs while Ms. Perez watched. None of the Latino mothers allow the younger children to get too far from their view for too long. While the Latino children observed do not seem to have the same level of discipline provided by a parent as the black students I studied, they are watched more closely. It may be that they have less latitude so less discipline is necessary. If this is the case, one wonders what will happen as they grow up and more latitude is required or demanded. Will they have the discipline necessary to handle the freedom?

After playing for a while, Alex, Annette, the two children from downstairs, Ms. Perez, and the observer returned to the house, and Annette and Alex asked to play outside. After a bit Ms. Perez called both of them in to do their homework. Alex responded that since it was a Friday, he did not have much homework and that he had already completed it. His mother then told them both to take a shower. In the black homes in which the children do well, the mother insisted upon seeing the completed homework every day, while Ms. Perez accepted her son's word. While his word may indeed be good, when the parent checks the work, the student sees an even higher level of concern. Asking is very important, but checking is even more helpful.

Alex had a baseball game at the time of the next visit, and the observer accompanied Ms. Perez and Annette to the game. When it was Alex's turn to bat, his mother gave him a "thumbs up" to wish him good luck. Alas, Alex struck out, but when he walked toward his mother, downtrodden, she encouraged him by saying that he would do better the next time. It is precisely this kind of parental support and encouragement that helps young people to build their self-esteem and sense of responsibility, both of which are crucial if one is to do well in school. In fact, without positive self-esteem it is very difficult to do well, given that one is likely to be corrected often in school. If self-esteem is low, the student may avoid school to avoid the corrections.

Alex was the only Latino boy on the team, according to his mother. We saw no evidence that this made him uncomfortable. Indeed, he seemed comfortable, though shy, both at band practice, where he is one of two Latinos, and around his ball team. This confidence will serve him well as he matures. This is, after all, one of the values of diversity. Alex's team won the game, which made him happy, and after snacks supplied by the players' families, the Perez family and the observer went back to their house. Alex commented that he was sorry that his father was not at the game, but that he understood that he missed the game because he had to work.

The observer arrived for the next observation as the family was eating dinner. When Alex finished his dinner, he went to the living room to watch television, followed by Annette when she had finished. When Mr. Perez finished his dinner, he went again to read one of the volumes of the encyclopedia, while the observer and Ms. Perez discussed the last few days of school for the children. Alex and Annette then brought portfolios made at their school for the observer and their mother to see. Alex's portfolio dealt with the field trips made by his class during the school year, while Annette's dealt with a story she had written throughout the year as she learned to read and to write new words.

Ms. Perez asked Annette to read her portfolio out loud. After a few sentences, she did her usual complaining about not feeling like reading anymore, but her mother insisted that she read a few more pages. She laughed hysterically, lost concentration, and quit reading at all. She seems to manage to get away consistently with not reading very much, and her parents do not seem to want to insist that she read more. Her father was known to compromise with her and therefore let her avoid much reading. It may not be the reading that is so important here, but the apparent lack of discipline on her part. On the other hand, she is young, and unlike most of the Latino children observed so far, she is at least encouraged by her parents to read and to show them that she is doing so.

As the children put away their portfolios and papers from the last day of school, Mr. Perez again began to read from the encyclopedia. When they had finished with the school materials, the children turned on the television to watch a cartoon show, but the noise distracted Mr. Perez, and they were told to turn the television off, which they promptly did. Mr. Perez explained that the show they were watching was not the type of show he wanted them to watch. Ms. Perez said that she prefers the shows on the local public television station because they are educational and therefore better for the children.

Alex then went off to shower, while Annette was asked by her mother to read another book. She did not, but she did read more from her portfolio before her mother bathed her after Alex had showered. When both children were clean and Annette's hair was combed, they played a board game on the kitchen table, while Mr. Perez discussed the goals of this research with the observer. He commented that he thought that any effort that might improve education for young people should be applauded. By then it was bedtime for the children.

The last visit took place after school was out for the year. When the observer arrived, the children were watching an educational show on the public television station. When the show was over, they turned the television off. Ms. Perez reminded them that they had joined a book club at the local library that required that Alex read thirty minutes, and Annette twenty minutes, each day at the same time during the summer. They each kept a log for each day of the time and number of pages read. After Alex discussed his book briefly with his mother, he and his sister decided that they would rather relax that day, so their mother suggested that they watch videos that they had gotten from Family Focus.

The first two videos were about science projects that could be done at home, and Alex showed a great deal of interest, even explaining the second video to his mother, after telling her that he had seen it before. As he explained the video, the observer noticed that he sometimes had trouble with some words, combining English and Spanish as he spoke, occasionally asking his mother for translation help when he could not think of a word he wanted to use in one of the languages. He had more trouble saying complete sentences in Spanish than in English. While this seems problematic now at home, it may serve him well in the future, since the school system and the larger society are unlikely to accommodate to a significant degree the use of Spanish only. Again, Alex has his mother to help him, while most of the other Latino mothers cannot do so. This, I suspect, alienates the parents from the institutions in which English is dominant and forces the children to grow up much faster because they must interpret and explain.

The children talked about the time they had spent earlier with their father. They visited the bank, and Annette talked about how much she enjoyed this because she received a free lollipop at the information desk. Mr. Perez seems to play a somewhat larger role in the upbringing and socialization of his children than other Latino fathers, though they are to a significant extent showing more concern about their children than did the poor black fathers studied. Mr. Perez is involved to some degree, not just concerned. Still, it is clearly Ms. Perez's job to care for the children.

When Alex went to the kitchen to get some cookies, he asked his mother if it was all right to eat them, something he had consistently done. As she had consistently done, Ms. Perez reminded him that it was common courtesy to offer what he was going to eat to any guests, namely, the observer. He is clearly being taught to be considerate of others, a valuable trait for school.

When Annette and Alex indicated that they were bored with the television and with reading, Ms. Perez reminded Annette that she had yet to do her twenty minutes of reading and that she had to do this before she could do anything else. While Annette reluctantly read, Alex played games on the computer, which is always kept on for fear that it will not come back on once it is turned off. Most of the games were educational games obtained from Family Focus. When he did well at a game, he expressed his happiness. When Annette finally completed her reading, they asked their mother to take them to the play lot. So, along with the two children from the basement, they walked to the lot.

Like most of the other children observed so far, the Perez children are courteous and well behaved. Like the others, they are closely watched by their mother. But unlike the others, they are not only very disciplined but also focused on school and educational activities, even when school is out. They are involved in activities outside of the home, and the parents make certain to teach them discipline, high self-esteem, cooperation with others, and to have high educational aspirations. Their home environment is orderly, structured, and quiet, allowing them to pay attention to their learning. The parents monitor their television watching and their play. Ms. Perez asks about schoolwork daily, and while she doesn't insist upon seeing the work every day, as do almost all of the parents of the higher-achieving poor black students, she does make certain that the children do the work. These parents seem to do almost all of the right things to prepare their children for school, including mastering English themselves, which is an enormous benefit for the children, no matter what one's position on the politics of the English-versus-Spanish argument.

THE FIGUEROAS

Mr. and Ms. Figueroa live in a small house in Evanston, in an area close to the home of the Perezes. The neighborhood has for a long time been composed mainly of poor and working-class blacks, but in recent years more and more Latinos have moved in. They have two children, nine-year-old Amy and four-year-old Jackie, and have lived in the United States for six years, all in Evanston. Like many of the Latinos studied, they have relatives in the area; ten of Ms. Figueroa's brothers and sisters live close to them. Both Mr. and Ms. Figueroa grew up in Mexico, and both reached the sixth grade in school. Like most of the other Latinas in the study, Ms. Figueroa is a housewife; Mr. Figueroa works in a factory. Ms. Figueroa believes that it is important that Amy receive an education, and she encourages her to do well in school.

She said that she offers verbal support but that she is limited in what she can do to help both by her limited education and by the fact that she doesn't speak English. These limitations make helping Amy with her homework difficult.

Ms. Figueroa visits Amy's school when there are activities and when it is required. The observer noted here that in her visits with the family to the school, Ms. Figueroa seemed to feel "isolated (by) the fact that she can't speak English and communicate with the teachers. Also, I didn't notice any of them doing an effort to reach (out) to her either."

Ms. Figueroa does not see anything that might interfere with Amy's ability to receive a good education, and she doesn't think that anyone tries to impede her success. Amy did mention, though, that sometimes some children harass her for being Mexican or for being a different color. Again, this does not seem to be an effort on the part of other students to hold Amy back in her academic efforts. Ms. Figueroa did say that she believed that her race plays a role in her life in Evanston but did not specify what this role was.

Both she and Mr. Figueroa are from a small, rural town in Mexico with no theaters and no cultural events. She said that she often tells Amy that she should do well in school in order not to end up like she is, uneducated and not very sophisticated.

While Ms. Figueroa stresses how important she believes the girls' education is, the observer pointed out that she saw very little discipline with the girls and that Jackie, particularly, seems "to be able to get away with whatever she wants." I have noticed that several of the younger girls are in the same position. As Morrison (1991) points out, preschoolers are often egocentric. This is one of the characteristics of preschool children that they must outgrow with the help of their parents. So, the younger children, especially the girls, are simply being preschoolers, but their parents must help them learn to be more cooperative, to share, and to delay gratification, and I do not see much help from the parents here.

Ms. Figueroa does not read newspapers or books, and she relies upon her family when she needs help. It is very difficult to convince the children of the value of reading when the parents do not read. And how can she read to Jackie, the preschooler, if she doesn't read at all? For the preschool child, being read to and trying to read are crucial activities.

Amy is in the third grade at a local elementary school. Her favorite subject is math. She is particularly fond of one teacher who seems to scold other children when they tease her because of her skin color or nationality. Evanston prides itself on its diversity—some of the residents refer to it as "Heavenston"—so this kind of teasing causes one to wonder about the real meaning and value of this diversity. Still, young people often just look for things to use to bother other young people, so it is unclear just how serious this harassment is. Amy most dislikes the fact that some other girls are mean to her because of her skin color and nationality. She also doesn't like some of the cafeteria food.

Amy believes that school is important and that she is doing fine in school. She does no homework on weekends, but she said that she devotes one to two hours a day to her homework during the week. She would like to go all the way to college and believes that this is possible. She doesn't read the newspaper, and she thinks that her family is the most important thing in her life. Her father helps her with her homework at times, as does her uncle, and she would like to have a brother in order to have "different experiences." She has her chance, because her mother is pregnant.

As is the case in most of the families studied, neither parent speaks English, leaving Amy to translate everything for them. When there is a school conference, Amy must translate what the teachers say to her parents. Her mother is aware that this causes stress for Amy because she cannot always get the translation correct. The bigger source of stress is, however, derived from the responsibility that this places upon Amy. She has to be both a child and an adult in some senses, because much of what the family does must go through her. Not only is it difficult for her parents to properly prepare her and her sister for school because of the communication barrier, but she must help them to deal with the larger society.

When the observer arrived for the first observation, Amy was completing her homework for that day. Ms. Figueroa mentioned that her husband had recently purchased a computer for Amy but that they were having trouble installing the games and programs on it. Small wonder, given that the instructions were likely in English. When the observer volunteered to help with the installation, she noticed that one of the programs translated Spanish to English, and Ms. Figueroa seemed very interested in this program.

The Figueroa home is small and on the second floor of a two-flat building. It has two bedrooms, a living room, a bathroom, and a kitchen. Amy's room is very small, and she has a list of things to do for each day of the week, including her household chores. She seems to be one of the few young people observed so far who has regular chores, if the list is any indication.

During much of the first visit, Jackie, the four-year-old, played by herself. However, near the end of the visit she began to talk to the observer a bit, mentioning her school and her friends, speaking both English and Spanish. She attends a prekindergarten class for a few hours a day in a bilingual school. While Jackie spoke both English and Spanish, Amy spoke mainly English. Rachael Grant (1995) writes, "In the case of very young learners, Garcia (1991) emphasized that preserving their cultural heritage is important to the identity and sense of well being for the children and their families" (p. 9). The language and culture provide "an important sense of self and family belonging" (Garcia 1991, 2).

This suggests that maintaining one's cultural heritage and language, or perhaps maintaining culture through language, allows the young child to feel more secure and therefore better prepared for learning. Then maintaining mastery of Spanish would be important to young Latinos in terms of education beyond the issue of language itself, and the fact that the parents speak only Spanish at home could be seen as advantageous. This, however, seems to assume that the larger society will understand, accept, and adapt to this, as opposed to asking the child to "integrate" linguistically and culturally into the broader society, as most American schools do. This is the very difficult and politically sensitive issue that must be addressed, and I will take up the discussion in a later chapter.

During the first two visits to the Figueroa house, the observer noted that the house is very small and somewhat messy. While there are two televisions, one in the living room and one in the bedroom shared by Mr. and Ms. Figueroa and Jackie, neither of them was on during these visits. At one point during the second observation, Amy mentioned that she wants to be a professional ice-skater. When asked whether there was an ice-skating rink nearby, she replied that there is but that her mother is too busy and too tired to take her to the rink. Not only would this be an excellent opportunity for Amy to become involved in an activity that she likes, but also, and more important, it would be an opportunity for her to become involved in the type of activity that helps with discipline, self-esteem, cooperation, and responsibility.

Amy began to look at the programs that had recently been installed on the computer. As Amy worked with the Spanish-to-English program, the observer noticed that she doesn't read Spanish very well. She mentioned that she is forgetting how to read Spanish. While this may help her in a non-bilingual educational environment, it could also pose problems with her parents, since she appears to be the one who must translate for them. Translating from English to Spanish may not be so difficult for her, but going from Spanish to English could be a problem. Further, to the degree that the Mexican cultural heritage is maintained through language, she may be in danger of losing that.

Mr. Figueroa works two jobs, but on this day he had not gone to the second job. He came into the living room and asked the observer whether Amy was doing well in school. Apparently, Mr. Figueroa had no idea of how well she was doing, though he is obviously concerned. Students in the primary grades in Evanston receive written evaluations, and the Figueroas have no way to read them, so it is difficult for them to know how Amy is doing, as Mr. Figueroa himself acknowledges, or what she might need to work on.

Neither of the Figueroa parents asked Amy about her schoolwork during the second visit. Mr. Figueroa spent a little time playing with the girls, the only time he has been observed spending time with them so far, though Amy said that it is most often her father who helps with the homework. Also, during this visit, the observer noticed that there is a second door off of the kitchen and had the impression that the door leads to a room that houses another couple. The observer has seen another young man and woman walk through the house. Again, these people could be a source of emotional support, as well as money, for the parents. Throughout this observation Jackie played in the house with several of her neighbors' children. Neither parent attempted to turn this play activity into a learning experience or use it to help Jackie develop cognitive skills, personal control, or linguistic skills.

During the next observation Ms. Figueroa asked the observer to explain to her the compact disc that she had received in the mail. It was a free offer from an Internet provider. I mention this only because it illustrates just how limited a family is when the adults cannot speak English. Young people all over America, and particularly in a city with a population as well educated as that of Evanston, not only know all about the Internet but use it almost daily. It has become a part of life in this country. The Figueroas, however, are shut out of this source of information, not necessarily because they cannot afford it, though that might be the case, but because they cannot understand it.

As Amy explored the computer, her mother told her several times that she, Amy, did not know how to do the things that she was trying to do. This is not particularly good for Amy's self-esteem. Amy indicated that she had no homework that day. There was some discussion about going outside since it was so hot in the house, and during that discussion Jackie came in from outside, had a snack, took a shower, dressed, and went out to play again. Mr. Figueroa arrived but remained only a few minutes before going off to his second job.

Ms. Figueroa, the observer, and Amy joined Jackie downstairs on the front porch while Jackie played with the neighbors' children. Jackie and the others played school, with Jackie playing the role of the teacher. She used a book to show the others the pages, talking in both English and Spanish. She made several trips upstairs to bring down more toys, but her mother told her to stop bringing them down since she was unlikely to want to take them all back up when she finished playing. Jackie then stood up and screamed at her mother that she was in fact going to continue to bring the toys down. The observer had "the impression that [Jackie] could get away with whatever she wanted."

While it is not uncommon for a three- or four-year-old to be self-centered, the parents need to help the child grow beyond this. It seems that a number of the Latino parents make little effort to do this, particularly with the girls. I have seen almost no effort to ask the children to behave in such a manner as to help them to develop the attitudes and characteristics so necessary in the school environment. Ms. Figueroa made no effort to help Jackie to begin to develop discipline in this situation, which really called out for it.

When the observer arrived for the next observation, Ms. Figueroa, Amy, and Jackie were in the living room preparing to go to Amy's school for an assembly that Amy had mentioned during the last observation. Mr. Figueroa was resting and, according to his wife, was not going to his second job until later. This may have given him the opportunity to attend the assembly, but he apparently elected not to do so. Before they left for school, the man who apparently lives in the back part of the house walked by carrying laundry. This was the third time that the observer had seen this young man, but when she was asked for the questionnaire how many adults live in the house, Ms. Figueroa answered "two." It may be that these persons are illegal and Ms. Figueroa does not want to acknowledge their presence. In any event, there is a discrepancy between the number of adults listed on the questionnaire and the number observed.

Once at the school, Ms. Figueroa introduced the observer to Amy's teacher, referred to by the observer as Amy's "professor." In fact, several of the observers, all of whom are Mexican Americans, and several of the older children observed referred to the teachers as professors, clearly a sign of respect for elders and teachers. According to Grossman (1995), this respect may prevent the student from challenging the teacher when such a challenge or disagreement is called for. It may also limit challenges to the teacher from the parents. The children and the parents may be nice and compliant, but that is not always a good thing, especially if the teacher is lax.

Amy's teacher said that Amy is doing well and is a smart girl. Amy and her family and one other family were the only Latinos in attendance at the activity, which was limited to Amy's class. Most of the other parents were "white, middle- [to] upper-class-looking with a few African Americans," according to the observer. When asked about this, Ms. Figueroa said that Amy was one of only two Latino students at this school. (The school does in fact have more than two Latino students; it appears that Ms. Figueroa was referring to the number in Amy's class.) She said that Amy had passed "the English test" that allowed her to attend the school. While Amy interacted with the other students, Ms. Figueroa stayed apart, isolated. She told the observer that she often "feels totally isolated from what is happening" because she cannot understand what is going on and cannot communicate with the other parents, the students, or the teachers. However, she goes to the events to show Amy that she supports her.

This kind of support certainly helps show Amy just how important school is and may help her place a high enough value upon education and her performance to do the things required to do well. The observer had the impression that Amy felt somewhat "embarrassed by her mom [concerned about whether] she were to do something inappropriate." Amy's embarrassment and her mother's feelings of isolation could well limit what Ms. Figueroa can do to show her support. The other Latino family was there and was "also relegated to a corner," according to the observer.

It is simply not clear how effective parents can be in properly preparing their children for a school experience that they cannot really understand because of both their lack of education and their inability to understand the language in which the lessons are taught and all of the instructions and advice are given.

The next visit was a short one because the observer arrived just before dinner and did not want to interfere. The observer and Amy talked a bit, once she returned from the store with her father. The conversation centered upon Amy's last few days of school for the academic year. Amy spoke in English to the observer when they were alone and in Spanish when her parents were present. This allowed her parents to understand what she was saying in their presence and was also probably a sign of respect for them. If she were to speak in English when they were present, it might be seen as an attempt to hide something from them, or to talk "above" them, and would be disrespectful in either case.

During the last observation, Ms. Figueroa asked the observer whether she could take Amy to the local indoor ice-skating rink so that she could ask about ice-skating lessons. The observer agreed and asked to take Jackie as well if she wanted to go. Once at the center they found that the classes had already begun but that Amy could still enroll. Amy was disappointed after finding out the cost, figuring that her mother would not allow her to enroll.

While at the local ice-cream parlor, the girls told the observer that Jackie had had her birthday the previous weekend and that they had gone to a favorite local children's restaurant to celebrate. Amy said that her birthday is December 15 and that she receives one present for both the birthday and Christmas. I mention this only to give readers some idea of what it is like to be a poor child. Amy has already come to accept that if the extracurricular activities that she likes cost money, she is unlikely to be able to participate. Further, she seems comfortable with the reality that she will receive one gift for both Christmas and her birthday. Still, poverty is not really an excuse for her parents to fail to do the things needed to properly prepare her and her sister for school. Many poor parents do the required things daily. The Figueroas apparently do not.

When asked by the observer about her grades in school, Amy answered that she had received A's and S's, which Amy explained are better than A's, but are in reality indications of satisfactory work. This suggests that Amy may not fully understand the grading system. It is clear that her parents cannot understand the system, and it appears that they do not understand the educational system itself. I do not believe that this is a function of their lack of income, though it may well be related to their lack of education. A sixth-grade education is not much schooling.

Amy said that she did not have to attend summer school, at least that she did not want to do so. However, Ms. Figueroa apparently wants her to go. They will know soon, because the school will send a letter if Amy needs to go to improve any skills. If such a letter arrives, Amy will have to read it to her parents and explain the logistics to them. Can we really expect these parents to properly prepare Amy for an experience that they have never had, from which they feel isolated, and for which they need an interpreter?

Amy said that during the summer she and Jackie go to the park, go swimming at the YMCA, and play with the neighborhood kids. As the observer prepared to leave, she felt a bit sad, as was the case for many of the observers, who sympathize with the plight of poor Mexican Americans trying to do well in a foreign land in a foreign language. She wrote, "I believe [that] it is obvious that her parents want their daughters to do good in school and get an education because it is going to help them in the future. The lack of their own education and understanding of English makes their efforts even more difficult, but in their limited situation they have tried to provide for their daughters' educational growth." This could have been written about most of the parents observed thus far. They all want the best, even migrating from Mexico to try to obtain the best for their children. However, they seem to fail to do their part, not so much because of the lack of money, but because of the lack of familiarity with the educational system and its needs and because of their inability or refusal to speak or read English.

THE MARADIAGAS

Mr. and Ms. Maradiaga, both from Mexico, have three children: ten-year-old Jesus, nine-year-old Randy, and their four-year-old daughter, Lucia. They live in a very small one-bedroom apartment in Evanston; they have lived in Evanston for five years. Mr. Maradiaga works in an auto body shop. Ms. Maradiaga does not work outside of the home and speaks only Spanish.

Both Mr. and Ms. Maradiaga completed the equivalent of high school in Mexico. Ms. Maradiaga said that she wants her two boys to go as far in school as possible but added that how far they go is up to them. Given the importance of parental aspirations and support for children, this seems to suggest rather low expectations on her part. She said that she talks to them about the importance of school and visits their school occasionally and that she does not see anything to stand in the way of their receiving a good education.

Ten-year-old Jesus is a fourth grader. He likes the after-school activities most about his school and least likes homework. Still, he says that school is very important to him because "I have to get a job when I grow up"—not a very high ambition, I would say. He said that he devotes about forty minutes a day to schoolwork, and when asked how far he would like to go in school, he said that he would like to go "really, really far, like to high school." Again, his academic expectations seem rather low when compared to those of poor nonwhite students who do well academically. Still, he is rather young, and it may be that as a fourth grader he is not at the age yet to think much about these things. This is the major reason that we did not administer the questionnaires to the younger children.

Like Jesus, nine-year-old Randy expects to go to high school. Randy wants to be a mechanic when he grows up, while Jesus wants to be a soccer player. Not much education is needed for these jobs, and these young men do not seem very concerned about, or interested in, education, judging by their answers to our questions. Their mother does not appear very concerned about, or interested in, their education either. Randy says that he devotes about an hour each evening to his schoolwork, and neither brother does schoolwork on the weekend.

Jesus and Randy sleep in a bunk bed located in the living room, which also contains a desk with a computer, a bookcase containing a number of children's books, and a table with "three chairs that is partially in the kitchen." There is a small television in the living room, but "other than that there is no other furniture in the house," save the parents' bed and Lucia's bed in the one bedroom. Five people in three rooms makes for a cramped situation. It also makes it very difficult to maintain the order, structure, and quiet that seem to really help children do better in school. There is no privacy for anyone. Where will the boys go to do their homework in an environment that allows them to concentrate? In the living room with the television? In the kitchen, which opens to the living room?

Indeed, the observer wrote about her first visit, "It was noisy in the house because the two boys were playing with their cousin Jose, who is eight years old, on the computer and the little boy that lives next door was over as well." Lucia was in the one bedroom playing with Jose's five-year-old sister, Meribeth. Every now and then, Lucia would peek into the living room to check on her brothers and the observer.

Ms. Maradiaga indicated that her husband works Monday through Saturday from 7 A.M. until 6 P.M. at the auto shop and that he has a very strong presence in the household. In fact, he does not want the children to go outside to play because there is only a very small play area in their apartment complex, and he doesn't want them to venture beyond the complex. She said that she occasionally "sneaks" and lets the children go out to play before her husband arrives home from work. If they see their father approach, they run inside before he sees them, and Ms. Maradiaga doesn't tell him that they were outside playing lest he become angry.

At one point during this visit, the three boys went into the kitchen, found the potato chips, and began to eat rapidly. Lucia then came into the kitchen, saw them eating, and shouted to her mother that she was angry that they ate the chips and did not share with her. She went back to the bedroom and slammed the door behind her. While this was an opportunity for Ms. Maradiaga to teach Lucia to delay her gratification, nothing of the kind took place. Furthermore, as is the case for so many of the preschool girls, Lucia threw a tantrum to get her way, and nothing was said or done about it. She learned nothing from the experience except that the tantrums are accepted by her mother, not a particularly good lesson in the school preparation process.

This didn't end with Lucia, however. Randy demanded more snacks from his mother, who offered him oranges, bananas, and milk, only to have him reply "That sucks" every time she made an offer. He finally accepted a cup of chocolate milk.

Ms. Maradiaga then told the boys "about fifteen" times to turn the computer off. Each time, Randy replied "That sucks" or "Shit." According to the observer, the children "seem very comfortable telling her what to do." This is an unusual sign of a lack of respect for their elders. While I have seen this from most of the younger girls, it is unusual to see it with the older children. It could well be related to what appears to be Mr. Maradiaga's heavy-handed way with the children and with his wife. Perhaps his presence is so strong that hers is diminished to the point that they pay her little attention. This would be a serious problem since she is the one who remains home and is expected to be the principal caretaker for the children.

After the tussle over the computer, Jesus sat down on the floor next to the observer to take out his homework and some papers from school to show to his mother. After reviewing them, he handed two of them to his mother saying, "Here, Mom, these are the important ones for you to read." So, the ten-year-old decided for his mother just what was important coming from school. He began a reading and spelling assignment but paid little attention to the work, in part because his cousin Jose bothered him until he threatened to get up and "kick [his] butt." Not only does he show little patience, but also he shows little control over his mouth and emotions and is prepared to settle his disputes through conflict rather than through negotiation or cooperation.

Children fight, but it is up to parents to teach them alternatives to conflict. If they don't, teachers have a very difficult assignment, one for which they are really not prepared and for which they are certainly not paid.

While this was occurring, Randy went to bathe rather than to start his homework as his mother requested. When he finished, he asked his mother for permission to go outside to play. She told him no, but he went anyway! He simply ignored his mother. Do we expect him to pay much attention to a teacher? At no time did Ms. Maradiaga inquire about the boys' homework, look at the work, or try to help them with it.

Soon Ms. Maradiaga's sister arrived to pick up her children, just as Lucia, who seemed bored, went outside as well, telling her mother as she left, "I'm going outside. I have one foot outside of the door already." So, Jesus did little homework, Randy did none, and Lucia did whatever she wanted to do.

There was no mention of homework at all during the next observation. Jesus had just gotten out of the shower when the observer arrived, and Ms. Maradiaga told the observer that the family needed to shower or bathe earlier in the day because there was often no hot water later in the day. Again, the cousins were over, and all three of the boys played on the computer as the girls, Meribeth and Lucia, played in the bedroom. When the boys tired of the computer, they shut it off and went to the kitchen to eat ice cream, without Ms. Maradiaga's permission. In fact, when Jesus offered the observer ice cream, which she declined, saying that she needed to cut down on her sweets, he remarked to his mother that she should do the same thing! This is a ten-year-old telling his mother what she should and should not eat. Where is the discipline? Where is the much vaunted respect? Where is the self-control?

Jose began to tell the observer how he had had to make a presentation in school that day and had been nervous about it. He did not talk to his aunt about this. The presentation was his autobiography, which he had written in a book that he then used for the presentation. Jesus and Jose then sat down to read different books, both in English, but were bored after ten minutes and went to the bedroom to harass the girls, who promptly told them to get out.

Later, Ms. Maradiaga told the observer that once a month a social worker, sent by Family Focus, comes to the house to "work with Lucia and to play games [and] activities with her." According to Ms. Maradiaga, Lucia does not "open up" to her, even though she has been coming for a while now. In fact, Lucia told her mother on the social worker's last visit that she didn't want to play with her anymore.

When the observer next arrived at the Maradiaga house, the three boys were doing their homework, while Lucia was, as usual, in the bedroom with Meribeth, playing. Actually, it is a bit of a stretch to say that all three boys were doing their homework initially, because Jose had difficulty finding his, given the mess in his book bag. Jesus was, however, sitting on the floor "struggling" with a math assignment and calling his mother for help every few minutes. While she tried to help, she was increasingly frustrated because she did not really understand the fourth-grade math that he was doing. However, she tried, which, if done correctly, could send a positive message to Jesus. However, with his cousin and brother sitting on the floor with him, also struggling and making noise, and his mother making no effort to let him know how important the work and his efforts are, it is not clear that this was either a good environment or a positive effort on the part of Ms. Maradiaga.

Soon, as should be expected, Jesus became frustrated and paid little attention to his work. His mother paid no attention to this shift. Ishmael, a neighbor and friend of the boys, arrived and, after being asked by Jesus, helped with the homework, which he described as "easy." When the work was complete, thanks to Ishmael's help, Ishmael suggested that they go outside to play. Randy put his work aside and went with Ishmael, after telling his mother in response to her inquiry that his work was complete. She told him that he could not go outside until his work was done, but he ignored her and went anyway.

While this was going on, the girls were in the bedroom listening to books on tape, in Spanish, which had been checked out of the local library. They listened to "Goldilocks and the Three Bears" before Jose began to bother them. They then went to the kitchen to avoid him and to have a snack. The boys went to play, after showering and bathing, while the girls sat with Ms. Maradiaga and the observer in the living room fussing and shoving one another. When Ms. Maradiaga noted their confrontational "play," Lucia responded, "We're playing over here on our own, so don't bother us."

This contrasts sharply with what I recall of a four-year-old poor black boy in one of the families I studied (2002). He did not answer swiftly when his mother asked whether he had completed his chore for the day, which was to clean the toilet bowl. When his response was not quick, his mother told him that she was going to check to see whether he had done the work and that if he had not, she was going to clean the bowl "with [his] head." While she laughed later, she was serious, and he immediately went to clean the bowl. His sister, the student being studied, was an honor student who did her homework as soon as she arrived home, then did her household chores, and then completed any remaining homework before she could go to bed.

When her mother arrived from work every day, she wanted to see the children's schoolwork, discuss their day with them, and check on their chores. This was in fact the daily schedule for almost all of the students who did well in school. I cannot imagine Lucia or Jesus surviving to tell the tale in this household after saying some of the things they said to their mother. Nor can I imagine them doing well in school given the way they are being raised, or perhaps I should say the way they are not being raised.

Ms. Maradiaga responded to her daughter's rebuke with a laugh. When the observer asked Lucia questions about the books she and her cousin were reading, Ms. Maradiaga said, "Lucia doesn't even know how to read"—not particularly good for her self-esteem. Lucia responded, "Yes, I do, so shut up." The mother made no effort to establish discipline, and the girls sat down to eat popsicles.

The boys then returned from outside and asked permission to go to the park to play soccer. Ms. Maradiaga granted the request, after letting the observer know that she did not allow the children to play with just anyone, but their cousin was acceptable. Soon, the girls went out to play as well.

During the next observation, the boys played Nintendo in the bedroom, while Meribeth and Lucia played in the living room with dolls, paying little attention to the television, which was on. After Meribeth's mother came to take her children home, Lucia mentioned that she had been given an assignment earlier that day at Family Focus. She had several worksheets to complete, each one concerning the alphabet. One had to do with matching objects with the letter of the alphabet with which the name of the object began. She struggled with this one for a time, while her mother, sitting next to her, offered no help and no encouragement. The observer explained to her what she needed to do, and she completed the assignment.

The boys were wrestling on the floor next to Ms. Maradiaga, the observer, and Lucia while Lucia worked on the assignments. This is not a particularly good environment in which to learn. While Ms. Maradiaga told the boys to stop numerous times, they continued, telling her that they were bored and that wrestling was fun. Again, the boys did what they wanted despite the protestations of their mother, and again she did nothing other than ask them to stop. Once again, they did no schoolwork, and their mother did not ask about school.

After the boys decided to cool off by taking a shower, Mr. Maradiaga arrived home from work. This was the first time that the observer had seen him in the three weeks she had visited the home. There was no evidence that he played any real role in the upbringing of the children or their preparation for school.

When the observer arrived for the next observation, Jesus and Randy were sitting in the living room watching television, along with their cousin Jose, while Lucia and Meribeth, as usual, were in the one bedroom, also watching television. The boys began to talk about who had to attend summer school—school was out for the year—and Randy indicated that he had to attend to work on his English because he was being moved to a regular English class the next fall. Jose said that he had received no paperwork regarding summer school, so he assumed that he did not have to attend. He was happy because he was leaving for a month in Mexico when his mother arrived from work that day.

After Ms. Maradiaga's sister came to pick up her children, Randy and Jesus continued to watch *The Simpsons* on television, and Lucia sat at the kitchen table with the observer. During the discussion about summer school, Ms. Maradiaga said nothing, almost as though she has nothing to do with the boys' education.

A little later Mr. Maradiaga arrived home from work, and talked with the observer about higher education. He noted that it made him happy to see Latinos in universities. Since this observation and the next three all took place after school was out for the boys, we have an opportunity to observe the family environment at different times of the day and under different circumstances. Do we see the discipline needed for good school performance? The development of cooperation? The focus on high educational aspirations? The internal control? The future orientation? Is Lucia learning to take direction, to work by herself, to listen to others, increasing her vocabulary, learning space and time concepts? These are all things that preschoolers need to have mastered when they enter school, things that help them do better in school.

We know that she knows how to use some words, given that she referred to Jesus as a "dumb ass" when her brothers had a brief spat over who would get what snacks bought by Mr. Maradiaga.

During the next visit, Lucia, Ms. Maradiaga, and the observer had a brief discussion about babies as a result of a television commercial they were watching. Ms. Maradiaga explained that she had been pregnant a year ago and had carried the baby for seven months before a miscarriage. During the pregnancy, Lucia had picked out a name, Pedrita, for the baby. When asked by the observer whether she would use that name for her child when she was old enough to bear children, she responded that she was not going to have children because it hurts. She explained that she learned this from the worker at Family Focus. She said that her mother was going to have her children for her because she wanted to avoid the pain.

When the boys emerged from the bedroom after playing video games complaining that they were hungry, Ms. Maradiaga asked what they wanted to eat. Jesus wanted a sandwich with toasted bread, lettuce, tomato, cheese, and avocado; his mother quickly prepared it for him. Of course, it is not his eating preferences that are important here but his mother's rapid response to please him. She seems to go out of her way to please all of the children, and they seem to expect to be pleased—an expectation that will often go unmet in the school environment.

While Jesus ate his sandwich and watched the small television in the living room, Randy asked for *chicharones*, which are fried pork skins. His mother "immediately" got them from the refrigerator and began to fry them. The observer wrote in her notes, "I thought wow, if I would have asked my mother for all of this stuff, she would have killed me. But Ms. Maradiaga very patiently prepared the kids' lunches and even made them fresh lemonade; she seems to enjoy doing everything that she does for them."

While the family watched television after eating, Jesus fell asleep on the floor until he was awakened by his brother, who was hitting him on the head with a Styrofoam tube. Ms. Maradiaga told Randy to leave Jesus alone; Jesus went to lie on the bed, and the others returned to watching television.

When the observer next arrived at the Maradiaga household, the boys and Lucia were in the bedroom playing—actually, the boys were acting as though they were beating their sister up. When asked why they were doing this, they gave their "favorite" response, that they were bored. When asked how summer school was going, Randy said that it was going fine, and Jesus replied that he was happy because he had already missed two days: the day before because he didn't know which school to attend, and that day because he missed the school bus. Both boys said that they liked summer school because they were not as bored as they were at home. It is difficult to understand how their parents could be so lax with respect to their education that Ms. Maradiaga wouldn't know which school her son should attend or make certain that he was ready for the school bus. Further, the fact that both boys had to attend summer school suggests that they were not as prepared in some area or areas as they needed to be. Neither their mother nor their father seemed particularly concerned about this.

When the ice-cream truck came past, all three children asked Ms. Maradiaga for money to buy ice cream. She responded immediately, giving the boys five dollars and telling them to buy five ice-cream bars. As they ate the ice cream, Lucia informed the observer that hers was better because it was lemon and lemon was the best, arguing with the observer, who told her that hers was orange and it too was good.

Meanwhile the boys watched cartoons and discussed what they watched with the observer. Jesus was more thoughtful about what they watched than his brother. All they did for much of the day was watch television. When we observed the homes of the poor black students who did well in school, they almost never watched the television, even on weekends.

The next visit began with watching the boys play video games, as usual, in the bedroom, Ms. Maradiaga making lemonade, and Lucia watching her mother and arguing with her over whether or not she, Lucia, ever liked to take naps. Lucia told her mother that she did not like the lemonade that her mother was making because she used green limes rather than her preferred yellow lemons; she repeated her preference for the yellow lemons several times. This sounds like the kind of self-centered behavior common among preschoolers, behavior that parents need to work to have the child move beyond. Learning to cooperate and to compromise is very important, and the parents must play a role here. These parents do not.

In fact, we did not see either parent work with any of the children on the skills or knowledge that they need in school much at all during the eight visits to the Maradiaga home. While Lucia watched the television in the living room, the boys played video games in the bedroom. While watching *Barney* on television, Lucia, responding to questions from the observer, discussed a new character on the show before going to the kitchen to ask her mother to read to her. She had gone to the library with her mother after leaving Family Focus earlier that day.

Her book bag was full of books, and it seemed that she had checked out the entire series of ¿Quien Soy Yo? a series of Spanish books. She asked her mother, who said that she was very tired, to read *Babar* to her. Ms. Maradiaga complied. The observer asked Lucia why, since her mother was tired, she did not read the book to her mother. Lucia said that she did not know how to read, she only knew the alphabet, but that when she started school (apparently in a few months), she would learn to read.

Evanston, while diverse in many ways, has a highly educated population; it is home to Northwestern University and adjacent to Chicago. Many of the parents in Evanston make certain that their children not only read, write, and count before they go to school but also that they have computer skills and have traveled to different places often. Children like Lucia will began school at a disadvantage, and her parents do not seem to even be aware of this. I have seen nothing to suggest that they know at all how to deal with this, though their attendance at Family Focus does suggest that Ms. Maradiaga may feel the need for help. Language does not seem to be a huge problem in this house. The boys are, however, attending summer school in part to improve their English skills, and Lucia is having books read to her in Spanish rather than English. This will not help her in school.

None of the Maradiaga children seems to have to perform household chores, and neither of the boys participates in extracurricular activities. These are activities that help to develop the discipline, positive self-esteem, ability to cooperate, and sense of responsibility that are critical in the school environment. Their parents say little and do even less to shape a future orientation or foster high educational aspirations in their children. These are not children who are being prepared for school by their parents. It may be that the parents are struggling to make a living and to adjust to a different language, a different life, a different place. It may be that they simply have no idea of what to do or how to do it. Other poor folks manage, however, to know what to do and to do it. Poverty is not an explanation, or at least not a complete explanation, though it certainly is a barrier.

THE CHAPAS

The Chapa family is somewhat different from the others observed. Both Mr. and Ms. Chapa have college degrees. Ms. Chapa has a law degree, and Mr. Chapa is the general manager of a manufacturing company. Why look at such a family when I am studying poor Latinos? Ms. Chapa, like the others observed, takes advantage of the services and help offered by Family Focus and wanted to participate in the study. More important, it is an opportunity to compare to a small extent the poor families with a nonpoor Latino family in terms of what goes on in the home that may contribute to, or detract from, the preparation of the children for school. I will not dwell too much on the Chapas given that they are not really the kind of family that I wished to observe, but the contrast and comparison may be useful and should be interesting in any event.

The Chapa family is the only family studied in this or my earlier research in which the father was the one to complete the questionnaire, despite the discussion of the dominant role of the male in many Latino households. It is, of course, the only family in which the father is a professional. In all of the other Latino households, the father was at work when the questions were being asked. In several of the black households, however, the father was at home, but the mother elected to answer the questions. In this case, even though Ms. Chapa does not work and was therefore available, her husband answered the questions.

The Chapas have lived in Rogers Park, a community just south of Evanston in Chicago, for twelve years and in their current house for eleven years. They have three children: Anthony, who is six years old; Ari, who is three years old; and their sister, Gardenia, who is two years old. Mr. Chapa is from Peru, and his wife is from Mexico. Ms. Chapa speaks virtually no English. Mr. Chapa received a bachelor's degree in engineering. He said that the children's education is very important, because "it's the best legacy that I can leave them." He said that he tries to encourage his children to do well in school and is very active in doing so.

He encourages them by "instilling courage, building self-esteem, helping with homework, reading to them, and playing with them." This almost sounds like something from a textbook on effective parenting! He doesn't believe that there is enough support for the children in school, and he wants more help for them from the schools so that they can be bilingual. He describes his childhood as "good—best times of life. Different from now—didn't grow up as fast." He and his eight siblings were raised by a single mother. He believes that discipline is a key to receiving a good education. He reads a newspaper once a week, but he is "always reading" books. He relies upon his wife and family when he has a problem, and while he believes that there are many opportunities in the United States for his family, he believes that "language is an obstacle."

The observer first met Ms. Chapa at Family Focus, as was the case for the other participants. Ms. Chapa talked a great deal about the value of education and the parenting classes that she takes to help her children. The first meeting at the home took place on a Friday afternoon. The observer noted that the neighborhood seemed to be neat and the houses "well kept." The interior of the house was "clean, except for a few toys, and well kept." The rooms were "nicely furnished," and there were paintings on the walls in the living room and dining room. The kitchen had artwork done by the children on the walls. The house is a two-story home with a living room, dining room, television room, kitchen, bathroom, and foyer on the first floor. They have a piano in the dining room, as well as a small desk used by the children for their schoolwork. There were no books in sight. This sounds very different from the cramped Maradiaga home. Indeed, it is very different from the homes of any of the other Latinos or blacks studied. On the other hand, the Chapas are clearly middle-income folks, so we should expect some material differences.

During the observer's first visit to the home, Ms. Chapa was on the phone in the kitchen while a family friend waited for her, sitting at the breakfast table. Anthony also sat at the table counting Goldfish crackers one by one. Soon his mother got off the phone and told him to hurry because it was time for him to do his homework. But before he could do that, he was told to clean up the mess he had made with the crackers using a broom and a vacuum. When he did not do the job to her satisfaction, Ms. Chapa had him repeat the cleaning process.

One of the characteristics of the homes of poor blacks whom I studied (Sampson 2002) whose children were academically successful was that the children almost always had household chores to do. I have not seen this often among the poor Latino households. It appears that the mother, who is almost always a stay-at-home mother, does almost all of the household chores. It is true, however, that the children in these households are young, and one could argue that they are too young to perform these chores. Yet, here we have six-year-old Anthony cleaning up after himself with a broom and vacuum. Is it ever too soon to begin these lessons?

Ms. Chapa explained to the observer that Anthony has a snack when he arrives home from kindergarten and then does his homework in the dining room at his desk with his mother sitting with him for an hour. The hour is timed with an oven timer. When the timer goes off after an hour, Anthony can watch the only television show that he is allowed to watch, *Digimon*, for a half hour. Ari and Gardenia are upstairs napping while this transpires. On this visit, when they awoke and came downstairs, the two boys began to wrestle in the living room, while Gardenia sat in her high chair in the kitchen. When the boys began to make a lot of noise while disagreeing over something, Ms. Chapa scolded them for fighting and sent Anthony to his room as punishment.

This sounds very different from what we have seen in the Maradiaga household, where the boys often push and tussle, argue and disagree. Ms. Chapa apparently allows no loss of discipline. She also works with Anthony on his homework, something we have seldom seen among the other Latino mothers, and she maintains a schedule for Anthony, another characteristic of the households of academically successful children and something we have rarely seen among the Latino families studied to this point.

Ms. Chapa indicated that she usually takes the children to the local YMCA or a local park after dinner and that they are all going to the Mexican Fine Arts Museum the next day, a Saturday. Note that Anthony was doing his homework on a Friday, a day on which relatively few children do homework.

When the observer arrived for the next observation, Anthony let her in. Clara, a family friend who cares for an infant and is at the Chapa home daily, sat down with him when he returned to his homework in the dining room, helping him with his reading.

When Ms. Chapa arrived a little later, she took over from Clara with Anthony. At his school, work is done in both English and Spanish. Ms. Chapa speaks only Spanish, so the children hear only Spanish from her, but Anthony also speaks English. While this will help him in school, Ms. Chapa is at something of a disadvantage when it comes to helping him with schoolwork, but the effort is probably more important than the substantive help. She may well soon be at a disadvantage in dealing with school personnel if they speak mainly English. As Anthony worked on his schoolwork, his mother occasionally stopped him and asked that he discuss what he is reading. Clearly, she is very involved in his schoolwork and impresses upon him the value of that work.

When the timer went off indicating that it was time for the television show, Anthony was not finished with his schoolwork, so his mother did not allow him to get up from his desk. He became distracted and began to play with some toys, but Ms. Chapa took them away, explaining that when he studies, he cannot do anything else. While this may sound rigid, it is precisely the kind of order, structure, and discipline that I found in the homes of the academically successful poor black students and Furstenberg et al. (1999) found in the homes of successful urban adolescents. It appears to be just what is needed, but I have not often seen it in the other Latino homes.

Ms. Chapa asked Anthony to show her just what he did at school that day and to explain it to her. When the work and explanations were complete, Anthony put his books into his book bag and placed the bag in its designated location. Everything in order.

Anthony was now allowed to watch *Digimon*, but just before his half-hour time allotment was up, his mother told him that the television is about to be turned off because the time was about up. Anthony changed the channel in an effort to trick her, but she caught him and told him to turn the television off because the other children would be awake soon and she did not want them to watch television. When Ari and Anthony began to wrestle and fight again, she calmly told them that they "do not hit in this house," helping the boys to develop what Comer (1993) refers to as "personal control" and "interaction with others," both skills critical to good school performance.

At the time of the next visit the children were joined by Ricardo, a family friend who is seven years old. While eating dinner, the children caused a commotion. Anthony played, and Gardenia said that she did not want to complete her meal. Ms. Chapa told them all that they must finish eating and calm down if they want to go the park after dinner. When Anthony too said that he did not want to eat because he did not like the food and then because he was too full, she said, "Fine, I guess you're too full for dessert then too." He finished the meal.

When the children are finished eating, they must wash their hands, brush their teeth (Ms. Chapa explained to them why this is important), take their dishes to the sink, and clean up anything spilled on the floor or table. Again we see the order, discipline, responsibility, and structure characteristic of middle-class households that properly prepare their children for that middle-class institution, school. In this case we see them in a middle-income home, but they are certainly not restricted to this income level.

After dinner the children changed into clean clothes and prepared to go to the park. Before helping her, Ms. Chapa encouraged Gardenia, the two-year-old, to try to put on her own shoes. She seems to look for opportunities to encourage independence and thought on the part of the children.

While at the park the children played relatively freely, with their mother monitoring but not interfering. Soon, Ricardo's mother, who is African, came to pick him up, and the observer noticed that she and Ms. Chapa had something of a difficult time communicating, since Ricardo's mother does not speak English very well and, of course, Ms. Chapa speaks almost no English. Still, they managed, and after a time all returned to the Chapa home to find Mr. Chapa home from work. He is also very patient with the children and encourages them to think for themselves. When Anthony had a temper tantrum, yelling, "I don't want to do that," his father calmly asked, "Okay, just what would you like to do then?" He did not yell or scold, but neither did he allow the aggressive behavior.

While we made several more visits to the Chapa household, we observed much of the same. Ms. Chapa is patient but always looking for a way to teach the children even little lessons, like how to put on their own shoes. She asks Anthony about school every day and works with him on his homework every day. She insists that the boys clean up after themselves and tells Gardenia that she will not be allowed to have dessert unless she eats all of her meal. The self-control, sense of responsibility, discipline, structure, order, stress on the importance of education that are seen in so many middle-income homes in which the children are successful in school are all in evidence here every day. But this is a middle-income household, and the fact that it is a Latino household would seem to be an issue only with respect to the limitations imposed by Ms. Chapa's inability to speak English. A number of the poor Latino households observed for this work exhibit few of these characteristics, and some show some of them, but in none have we seen what we see in the Chapa household.

4

FINDINGS AND ANALYSIS: WHAT HAVE WE LEARNED?

We know that poor urban students in general, and poor urban minority students in particular, perform less well in school at all levels than their suburban, nonpoor, white counterparts. Myriad efforts have been tried to deal with this achievement "gap," none with much success. Some of these attempts would be almost comical were the subject not so very serious. Chicago, a city whose school population is some 85 percent nonwhite, mostly black and Latino, and overwhelmingly poor, has in the past dozen years tried greater parental and community control over the schools in response to this problem, only to turn around some six years later and concentrate control in the hands of the mayor. Neither effort has been accompanied by significant improvement in the school performances of any significant number of poor Latino or black students.

A host of cities are trying increased standardized testing, apparently reasoning that if students are tested more, they will learn how to do better on the tests and eventually will do so. Cities are trying vouchers, charter schools, longer school years, the wearing of uniforms, and the cessation of social promotions—that is, the passing of students to the next grade even though their performance in class suggests that they are not yet ready for that grade. They apparently give little thought to how a fifteen-year-old will feel in a class with only twelve- and thirteen-year-olds and what the student will do as a result of those feelings. Now, I am not a supporter of social promotion, but many thoughtful people would tell these school systems that they are pushing many of these students out of school prematurely.

It appears to me that none of these "solutions" is a panacea for this serious and growing problem. We simply cannot continue to fail to support generation after generation of the students who are most in need of a quality education, yet we continue to try methods that we should know at the start have little chance of lasting success. However, some of these poor minority urban students do quite well in school, and in life after school, while many more do not. If we could understand why some can do well, perhaps we could figure out just what we need to do with and for the others to improve their chances of academic success. This is what I set out to do in my research. I started from the premise that "all young children have the basic intellectual skills and the potential to learn" (Bempechat 1998, 2), with the possible exception of those with learning disabilities and retardation. Thus, somehow changing intelligence or giving up on those whom others might think to be "slow" was not an issue for me, unless "slow" means retardation or learning disabilities.

Given the growth of the Latino population in cities such as Washington, D.C., Los Angeles, Chicago, Miami, and Denver and throughout the state of Texas, I wanted to study what happens in the households of poor Latinos that might affect the learning of the students in those homes. Why focus on households? The work of Clark (1983), Furstenberg et al. (1999), Comer (1993), Harrington and Boardman (1997), Bempechat (1998), Morrison (1991), and Grossman (1995), as well as my own earlier work (Sampson 2002), suggests the primacy of the family in preparing the student for school.

Furstenberg et al. (1999) emphasize the importance to educational success of parental warmth and parents' promotion of the child's autonomy, and of discipline. Bempechat (1998) stresses that parents should maintain high educational expectations, encourage positive self-esteem, strengthen home-school partnerships, set education as a top priority, and allow children to "suffer" through hard school- and homework. Clark (1983) found that the high achievers in his research had homes in which the parents had frequent contact with schools, were calm with the children, expected to be actively involved in the child's education, and provided nurturance and support and in which the students learned to accept norms. Comer (1993) points out that parents should help the children learn to interact with others, learn personal control, differentiate between right and wrong, and learn how to think, use language, delay gratification, and regulate impulses. Morrison (1991), focusing upon preschool children, stresses parental involvement in the child's education and with the child's teacher. He also lays out a series of goals for the preschool experience that clearly are affected by what goes on in the home. These goals include helping children get along with others; learn to care for their personal needs; develop a positive self-image; learn shapes, sizes, and colors; increase their vocabularies; and learn to think in a "Piagetian sense."

I found (2002) that the higher-achieving poor urban black students whom we observed had parents who stressed discipline, cooperation, internal control, high educational aspirations, responsibility, and a future orientation and had home environments that were orderly, quiet, and structured. Some of the lessons that the parents tried to teach centered around having the children perform household chores and the children's involvement in extracurricular activities, both of which emphasize discipline, cooperation, and responsibility.

The same qualities are present in the homes of high-achieving students whether the parents are poor or middle income. This should not surprise us since, as Comer (1993) tells us, school is an "instrument of the mainstream culture" (p. 305). Fortunately, many poor families are in fact middle class in terms of their values, worldviews, and approach to life. They prepare their children for school because they want to or because they know how to. In reality, I am not certain why some poor parents can, and do, do what needs to be done and others do not, but I know that it happens. This is a very good topic for further research.

Since I already had a good idea of what goes on in the home that helps the child to do well in school, the issue became the extent to which poor urban Latino families do these things and how they compare to the poor black families I had studied previously.

Bempechat (1998) speaks of "the Latino paradox" (p. 89). She found that while Latino students said that their parents stressed academic success, that they felt ashamed when they performed poorly in school, and that they related academic success to higher ability, they were quite low in academic achievement compared to Indochinese students who had the

CHAPTER 4

same beliefs. They seemed to have the mind-set necessary for success, but the success wasn't there. It is unclear to me based upon my observations that that mind-set is there, but it is very clear that there are serious obstacles for Latino students, the most notable being their parents' lack of English skills.

Virtually all of the mothers who agreed to participate in this research said that they did so in the hope or belief that it might help their children perform better in school, demonstrating a clear concern about their children's success. They were all very attentive, checking on their children, particularly the younger ones, if they were out of sight for a few minutes. Note that I wrote that the mothers agreed to participate. The fathers were present in all eight of the homes, a significant difference from the case of the twelve poor black families I studied earlier (Sampson 2002).

The presence of the husband allows the Latino mothers to concentrate on raising their children. They have the time for this, and presumably the energy, yet not all of them do it. While all of the Latino mothers indicated that the education of their children is very important to them, and all emphasized to their children the importance of respecting others, particularly older people, the discipline and sense of responsibility that parents need to help their children develop were often missing. For the most part, the children acted respectfully, but rarely did they have the designated time put aside daily for schoolwork or learning activities that I saw in the homes of the successful poor black children and in the home of the Chapa family, the middle-income, middle-class Latino family studied here.

While it is tempting to argue that this homework or study time that seems so important to the academic success of the poor black students may not be as relevant because most of the Latino students are so young, in the Chapa household, six-year-old Anthony is required by his mother to work and study for one hour, by the clock, every day. The Latino children seem to spend a great deal of time watching television and playing, time that could be spent on schoolwork or other learning activities.

Few of the children are involved in extracurricular activities. Eloise Ceja, the thirteen-year-old who is doing poorly in school, professed an interest in sports and the violin, but I saw no indication of her participation. Mr. Ceja was very involved with the life of Natalie, the twelve-year-old who was doing well in school. This involvement by the father was something rarely seen in the other Latino families, and almost never in the black families studied (Sampson 2002). Furthermore, the Ceja girls had household chores to do. Few of the other children observed had such responsibilities.

While these children were young and perhaps their lack of household responsibilities was a function of their age, young Anthony Chapa is expected to perform some of these chores, so age alone is not the explanation. I almost have the impression that the mothers are expected to care for the house and the children, the father is expected to work to make money, and the children are expected to go to school. The importance of certain interactions among these relationships seems lost for the most part.

The mothers, while attentive, rarely seem to interact with the children in ways that will help prepare them for school. There are of course exceptions. Ms. Gomez asked three-year-old Ellie to tell her the colors of the cubes with which she was playing, and when Ellie got the color right, her mother applauded her. Not only does this help to develop her self-esteem, but it also helps her in terms of her academic goals (Morrison 1991). Ten-year-old Alex Perez plays in an after-school baseball league, and his mother takes him to the games and to practice, staying to watch both. But when he does his homework, he does it alone. For the most part, the parents do not seem to pay the kind of attention to the children's learning and schooling that is needed.

Eloise Ceja shows a lack of interest in her schoolwork and in learning. While her parents are aware of this, they seem to say little and to do even less about it. While it is tempting to suggest that this is the result of a lack of knowledge due to poverty, a number of the poor black parents observed did seem to know what their children needed (Sampson 2002). However, several of the Latino mothers did not complete the equivalent of high school in Mexico, and few went to school in the United States, while almost all the black mothers observed completed high school. It may be that this difference in the mothers' educational experience limits their knowledge of what is required for their children to do well in this system.

Still, it seems to me that Ms. Maradiaga should have known that some sort of discipline was required when she told her sons "about fifteen times" to stop playing on the computer and to do their homework, only to have them ignore her until finally Randy, the nine-year-old, complied, muttering, "Shit, this sucks." If he will behave this way with his mother, how do we expect him to act with his teachers?

Ms. Perez received her GED in the United States, after completing the equivalent of the seventh grade in Mexico, so she has U.S. school experience and perhaps a better sense of what is needed in school. Her husband had only six years of school in Mexico but attends English classes at a local community college. He was often seen reading an encyclopedia, and Alex and Annette, the children, work on their schoolwork fairly consistently, though seven-year-old Annette seems to try to dodge her reading. At least her mother is aware of this and tries to ensure that Annette does her work. In addition to playing baseball, Alex also plays in the school band. This seems to be the model that works best in terms of children's academic performance. The students are disciplined enough to pay regular attention to schoolwork or learning activities. They are involved in extracurricular activities. Their parents provide a home environment that is conducive to studying and inquiry, and the children have responsibilities at home or in terms of extracurricular activities. The children are encouraged to think for themselves. Parents stress education and show their concern and interest by frequently discussing the school day and schoolwork with their children.

We see some of these actions in some of the poor Latino homes, but not all in any of them, and it is difficult to see differences among the parents that might explain the differences in their approaches to preparing their children for school. It is not that some have a great deal more education or money than others, save for the one middle-income family.

There is, however, an issue that seems to affect all of the families to some extent: language. Almost all of the mothers observed speak only Spanish. This has enormous implications for their ability to properly prepare their children for a school system in which the instruction is in English, the written information for the parents is in English, and the teachers for the most part speak only English. How do you help children with their schoolwork when that work is in a language you cannot understand? Why ask about the school day or day at preschool when you probably cannot understand much of what the child might say? If you are going to read to the younger children, do you do so in English so that the student hears or works with the language used in school? Not if you do not speak English.

While some argue that the educational system should change to accommodate the language difference (Sanchez 1997), it is not clear that this will happen soon, even if it should, and this is not clear to me. What about the children in the meantime? Garcia (1997) writes, "Culture and linguistic identity provide a strong and important sense of self and family belonging, which in turn supports a wide range of learning capabilities, not the least of which is learning a second language" (p. 2). Garcia suggests that caregivers and teachers should speak the same language as the child and "represent the child's cultural group" or become knowledgeable about the child's language and culture. While one or the other of these options is often in place in school environments that are heavily Latino, those that are largely non-Latino are unlikely to follow them.

Should the school system adapt, or should the family and children adapt? Grant (1995), citing Cummins (1986), argues "for considering the interplay between power relations and the language, culture of schools" (pp. 9–10). This is of course as much a political statement as an educational position, even though it may well be relevant educationally. The political dimension, however, suggests that folks who hold different political positions may attempt to stop or limit what may well make educational sense. I do not really take a position here. At this point the school system attended by all of the poor Latino students and in which the preschoolers live is overwhelmingly non-Latino and shows few signs of changing to accommodate the language or cultural differences of these parents.

Further, how are the children to prepare for a world in which most of the interaction is in English and the culture is predominantly non-Latino? Many of these children are in a bind, for they must grow up quite fast. They often serve as interpreters for their parents, putting them in position not only to interpret but also to explain educationally related topics and more adult issues as well. With that kind of pressure, education and school may often take a backseat. I am not at all suggesting that these parents learn English or drop their cultural heritage. That is not my position nor my place. I am reporting what I have observed and attempting to analyze those observations.

Some of the parents do some of the things that we know help preschool children when they enter school. Ms. Rangel reads to three-year-old Mary, and Ms. Gomez asked three-year-old Ellie to identify colors of cubes and to identify the animals and vegetables in a puzzle. She praised her when she went to the rest room alone. Still, with the notable exception of the middle-income Chapa family, I have not seen consistent efforts on the part of the parents to help the preschoolers develop the thought and educational skills that they will need in school. Indeed, on the whole the parents do not interact a great deal with the preschoolers.

Like the older children, the preschoolers watch a great deal of television, and with a few exceptions the shows are not the kind from which they are likely to learn much. Some families do the types of things known to help preschoolers, but none does them consistently. We know that poverty does not entirely explain these gaps in parental performance and household characteristics that lead to gaps in performance between poor and nonwhite students and nonpoor white students.

I have not seen much evidence of peer pressure on the students to limit their good performance, nor have I seen that these parents discuss the educational future with those students, as is often done in the homes of those who do well in school.

Further, while the fathers are present in all of the homes studied, they play virtually no role in the upbringing or preparation for school of the children, with the notable exception of Mr. Perez. They are there, but not much more. Grossman (1995) found high agreement among the Latino participants in his research for the position "In traditional Hispanic families, the father tends to function as the authority and decision maker while the mother is the nurturer and comforter" (p. 238). This would leave the mother to bear the burden of school preparation almost alone, and this is what I have observed.

The larger issue here, however, is whether there are cultural differences, of which the role of parents is just one, between Latinos and non-Latinos that have serious educational implications and might explain some of what I have found. Some have suggested that that is the case with black Americans: that they are culturally different from nonblacks in ways that negatively affect their classroom performance. Some have even suggested that blacks have a different language, Ebonics. This is of course a very contentious issue, with many black conservatives strongly opposed to that argument and others just as strongly in favor.

I have my doubts about the cultural argument as an excuse for failure. Indeed, I have my doubts about the cultural argument at all. If there is a black culture that is in conflict to some extent with the values and beliefs upon which American education is based, then why is it that we see none of this culture among middle-income or upper-income blacks? If it is "black," it should not be bound by income or education. Of course, this might lead some to suggest that those blacks who do not exhibit these "cultural" characteristics are not "black." This is, in my opinion, nonsense. Education in America is a middle-class experience, and middle-class blacks, whether they are poor or middle income, tend to do quite well in this system. Not as well as their white counterparts, but well. If anything, one could argue that there is a culture of poor blacks or, more precisely, of poor urban blacks.

Grant (1995) and Grossman (1995) seem to suggest that there is a Latino culture that seems to be in conflict to some degree with the culture that is taught and around which the American educational system is built. This, in their view, makes it more difficult for Latino students to do well. But there is no one single Latino culture. As Darder, Torres, and Gutierrez (1997) put it: "Unfortunately, these discussions have oftentimes been founded on myopic traditional perspectives which have engaged the Latino population in the United States as a monolithic entity. The consequence has been to perpetuate static notions of culture" (xiii).

There are Puerto Rican Americans, Mexican Americans, Central Americans, Latinos born in the United States, and Latinos newly arrived. They may share a language and many cultural characteristics, but not a uniform culture.

The characteristics that Grossman's (1995) Latino participants agree characterize a "Latino culture" include the importance of the family and group; respect for each other, and particularly elders; the importance of agreement; great respect for authority; the importance of learning by doing; pride and self-reliance; a notion of punctuality that differs from the Anglo concept; and a present orientation. He suggests that these characteristics will sometimes conflict with good school performance unless educators and school systems understand them and take them into account when teaching Latino students.

Of course some suggest that the Irish, the Germans, the black Africans, and the Polish who arrived here gave up their cultures in order to do well in this society and that the schools, as the major teacher of the culture of this society, simply did, and does, its job. By this reasoning, Latinos should give up "their culture," and their failure to do so holds back their performance. It has not held back the performance of middle- or upper-income Latinos. Do they give up "their culture" as the price of success?

This difficult and very sensitive issue should be confronted by those educators and educational policy makers who seek to make certain that poor Latinos have the opportunity to fare well in our schools. I did not see much evidence of a significantly different culture among the poor Latinos I observed that would significantly limit school performance. The parents' language limitations clearly affect what they can do for their children and how they interact with schools, and to the degree that cultural and linguistic identity are correlated, there may be other limitations here. I should note that Sanchez (1997) argues that the language difference need not be a hindrance to good education. For him, the issue is not language but "good schools."

It is my conclusion that the parents' lack of experience with the American educational system, their inability to speak English, and their recent arrival from poverty in Mexico are larger influences than culture. As in the poor black families I studied (Sampson 2002), some of the parents do some of the needed things sometimes, while others do few of them at all. This is borne out in the work of Clark (1983) and Furstenberg et al. (1999). Poverty itself is not the explanation, as some poor families exhibit middle-class values and characteristics.

I did not observe many completely middle-class families in this work. But for the most part, the families want their children to do well in school. It is very important to them. They just do not seem to understand the role they need to play to maximize the probability of this success. In terms of policy, it would be best to proceed from the assumption that parents who want the best for their children and are willing to learn can be taught to involve themselves in the lives and education of their children to improve their children's chances of academic success.

5

BLACKS AND LATINOS: ARE THERE DIFFERENCES THAT MATTER?

Bempechat (1998) tells us that "barring serious learning difficulties or mental retardation, all young children have the same basic intellectual skills and the potential to learn" (p. 2). This would suggest that we need to look beyond intellectual differences to determine why some poor minority children are well prepared for, and consequently perform well in, school, while many, perhaps most, of them are not prepared and perform poorly. The answer clearly is not poverty alone, given that some do well. The answer is not race or ethnicity: some blacks and other nonwhites do well. In 2002, I published the results of in-depth observations of twelve poor black families in Evanston in an effort to determine just why some poor black students performed well while others in the same schools, the same neighborhood, and at the same income levels performed poorly.

The differences that best explain the variation in school performance were the differences among the families and the resultant differences in the school preparation and characteristics of the children. Entwisle, Alexander, and Olson (1997), Clark (1983), Lareau (1989), and Furstenberg et al. (1999), among others, stress the impact of the family on the academic performance of students. In fact, Hurst (1996) states, "The involvement of parents in the education of their school age children is probably the greatest single opportunity for educational advance open to us today" (p. 105). This involvement is not simply attending parent-teacher conferences or PTA meetings but active involvement of parents in the *preparation* of their children for school. Clark (1983) argues, "Increased knowledge of the home functioning patterns in different ethnic communities will enhance the prospect of developing appropriate school policies and procedures for increasing the knowledge levels of all categories of school children, while preserving the integrity of 'the school' and 'the home' in each neighborhood" (p. 213).

In this work I wanted to determine the degree to which poor Latinos in the same community as the poor blacks observed possessed the characteristics so closely linked to academic success and the degree to which the parents do the things necessary to prepare their children for doing well in school. Finally, I wanted to compare the poor black and the poor Latino families in an attempt to gain some insight into the role of race and ethnicity in school preparation.

Stephanie Adams is one of the high-achieving poor black students studied; she receives mainly grades of A and B at her middle school. The Adams family migrated from Africa and have been in Evanston for seven years; they live on the west side of Evanston, the same area of the city that is home to all of the poor black and Latino families observed. Her mother, who helps Stephanie with her homework regularly, pointed out that she was raised in a very disciplined home and emphasizes discipline with her children. Stephanie's home is small, but orderly and tidy, and her mother demands that Stephanie and her siblings perform the household chores needed to keep it that way.

When Ms. Adams, whose husband is present in the home but was rarely seen during our weeks of observations, arrives from work each day, she wants to know how the school day went for each of her four children. Stephanie discusses her classes and her soccer practice almost every day. Each of the four children, even the preschooler, has a bank account. They are being taught planning, discipline, and order at young ages. At one point after arriving from work, Ms. Adams asked Stephanie's younger brother whether he had prayed that evening—they are Muslims—and when he replied "no," her response was "Now!" He immediately headed upstairs to pray.

During another observation, Ms. Adams asked who was doing the dishes that evening, and Stephanie answered that she was. One of the children had also prepared the dinner that evening. Before she could do her chores, however, Stephanie had to do her homework. In fact, all of the children had gathered around the kitchen table while they silently worked on their school-work. There was no television on, no radio on; no video games were played. Just homework. When Stephanie asked her mother to help with a math problem, Ms. Adams immediately tried to do so.

When the youngest boy bragged to his mother that he was using "TV time" to watch an educational show, Ms. Adams replied, "I have such a smart boy"—precisely the type of response that helps to boost self-esteem. At around 10 P.M. Stephanie complained to her mother that she was still having difficulty with her math, and Ms. Adams responded that the work was Stephanie's responsibility and that she must stay up until midnight if neces-sary to complete the work.

On another occasion, Stephanie and her older brother argued about who was to prepare dinner for the youngest child. The older brother lost the ar-gument and prepared the dinner, while Stephanie worked on her Spanish homework. When Ms. Adams arrived, each child discussed his or her day with their mother, with Ms. Adams asking frequent questions of each child. Stephanie discussed her tryout for the volleyball team, and one of the younger boys was asked (again) whether he had prayed. The routine seems to be the same each night: schoolwork, often involving the mother, prayers, and chores, though the order varies.

On one visit, when Stephanie's younger brother Fermi, a preschooler, showed off the drawings that he had done that evening, Ms. Adams referred to him as "the smartest boy in the world." His older siblings, to test "the smartest boy in the world," asked him various math questions. He answered all of them with absolutely no idea about what he was saying, but he tried, and they all laughed.

Even the preschooler is being challenged academically and praised for his accomplishments. This home exhibits all of the characteristics needed to help a student do well in school. Ms. Adams demands discipline and re-sponsibility, and she not only talks about the importance of school but demonstrates it by involving herself in the children's schoolwork and dis-cussing their days every day.

So does the family of Marie Thomas, another poor black student. She has a 3.00 grade point average as a freshman at one of the most demanding high schools in the country. Mr. Thomas watches the television a lot, and that sometimes seems to distract Marie. Still, she does her homework every evening after arriving home from basketball practice. She discusses her school day with her parents frequently and spends hours each evening on her homework. In fact during one observation, Marie moved from algebra, to history, to chemistry homework. On the day she received her grades for the academic period, her mother, obviously very proud, excitedly urged Marie to show them to the observer.

During that same observation, Marie indicated that she was fed up with her schoolwork. She had a biology test coming up, an English test as well, two essays due, and Spanish homework. Her mother suggested that she do some of the work that evening and get up early the next morning to complete it. When Marie continued to complain, she was told by her mother, "Get a grip on what [you have] to do." She was supportive and comforting but insistent that the work be done.

Fatima Robinson is another high-achieving poor black student living on the west side of Evanston and attending the same middle school attended by most of the poor blacks and increasingly by poor Latinos. Her grades are mostly A's and B's. During the first visit to the Robinson home, Fatima and her mother discussed how she might spend Friday night at the home of a friend. Her mother reminded her that she had a school commitment that night, before asking how her school day went. She then asked to see Fatima's homework before asking to see the homework of Fatima's ten-year-old brother and then offering to help with math homework.

During one observation, Ms. Robinson told the observer that if Fatima's grades fell when she went to high school the next academic year, she would be transferred to a local Catholic school, despite their lack of money. This suggests that she believes that Fatima controls her destiny. It also indicates that she is thinking about the future and is very concerned about Fatima's education. Fatima told the observer that she likes to do her homework as soon as it is assigned; she does not like to put things off. She listened to a CD for about twenty minutes, then turned it off and returned to her reading. Her two-year-old sister asked the observer to read to her, while Fatima read silently and her parents were in their bedroom watching television.

Fatima then warmed leftovers for dinner for her two sisters, indicating to the observer that she and her ten-year-old brother often trade off the household chores. After dinner, Fatima cleaned the kitchen and then returned to her room to read again. Her mother complained to the observer that too many parents in Evanston were not steering their children in the right direction, despite all of the opportunities in the city. This indicates that Ms. Robinson expects high performance from students and that she holds the parents at least partly responsible for their children's performance.

During a Sunday visit to the Robinson home, Fatima took part in a rally at the local high school to promote nonviolence and unity in Evanston, accompanied by the observer and her mother. Fatima tutors a younger child to whom she also donates her older clothes. This is a middle-school child! After the rally, they returned home, and Fatima showed the observer her latest math test, on which she had gotten a poor grade. When asked how her mother had responded, she replied, "Don't even get me started." Low scores are not acceptable in this household.

All three of these high achievers devote two to four hours a night to schoolwork, and all three expect to complete not only college but also graduate or professional school. Pierre Baroque, an average sixth-grade student who receives mostly C's and B's in school, also expects to attend graduate school. His mother believes that the only thing that stands in the way of his acquiring a good education is that he is sometimes "unorganized." She did not point to race or poverty or poorly trained or disinterested teachers. Rather, she placed the responsibility upon her son. His mother expects him to do well, and he, in turn, expects to do well.

Pierre lives in a small, two-bedroom house and shares a bedroom with his younger brother. During the first visit to their home, while Ms. Baroque prepared dinner, she asked Pierre what homework he had that day and asked to see his math textbook. At one point she told him that he needed to be better organized and to write neatly. While this was happening, Ms. Baroque prepared the younger brother's bath. When he indicated that he did not want to bathe, she made sure that he got into the tub anyway and that he stopped his complaints. On two occasions that evening Pierre asked his mother for help with his schoolwork, and she promptly turned to help him.

On another occasion he asked her for help with a word used in his science homework, and she told him to look up the word in the dictionary. When he used the word incorrectly in a sentence, she corrected him right away. So, she not only is closely involved with Pierre and his work, but she also urges him to be self-reliant. She is teaching him the importance of education and responsibility at the same time. Pierre wants to be a member of the basketball team, and his mother asked him often about his involvement with the team. He is also a member of the school band and wants to be on the student council. His grades hold him back both from the student council and the basketball team but not from his participation on the school newspaper.

During all of the visits to the Baroque home, Ms. Baroque, who, like virtually all of the black mothers observed, works full-time, emphasized quiet and order. During one visit Pierre was bothered by the noise being made by his younger brother. He began to protest the sound level with the sound "ffff . . ." but before he could say anything, his mother said sternly, "Don't say whatever you are about to say." "I was just going to say 'freak,'" he responded. "Don't say that," she scolded him. Harsh or crude words are not allowed.

Pierre confided to the observer that he is the best saxophone player in the band, an indication of his high level of self-esteem. His mother helped his younger brother with his first homework assignment from his kindergarten class, and we watched Pierre make a cake one Saturday, with a bit of help from his younger brother and his mother. He had to clean up the kitchen when he was finished with his baking, before carrying out the trash. Pierre is confident, disciplined, responsible, and cooperative: a nice, young, middle-class, poor black student doing fairly well in school despite living in poverty.

Tracey Love lives in the same neighborhood as the others with her father, mother, an older brother, and another adult. Her mother works full-time at a hospital. Tracey, whose grades are B's and C's, is involved with theater, the choir, basketball, and volleyball. She is a member of the church choir, takes piano lessons outside of school, and is involved in dance and drama outside of school as well. Her parents, like Stephanie Adams's, are immigrants, having come to the United States from the Bahamas eight years ago. So, these students' families were educated and raised in different cultures, have not been in Evanston very long, and yet the children do quite well in school.

Tracey, like the other high and average achievers, would like to go beyond college and attend graduate school. When asked which one person in the world she would be if she had the choice, she said she would like to be herself, "because I like myself and I am unique."

The first time that we visited Tracey's home, she was not at home. This was a Saturday, and this young lady is very busy on the weekends. Her mother called the Evanston Media Center, but she was not there. She found her at the local YWCA, where she along with others was practicing a song-and-dance routine. The next visit found her at home washing the dishes while her mother did paperwork at the kitchen table. The house was silent.

During another visit to Tracey's home, she was out again, this time practicing for a fashion show at Family Focus. This involvement in these outside activities helps to develop self-esteem, discipline, responsibility, the ability to cooperate with others, and internal control, all central to good school performance.

Tracey was a bit different from the other high and average achievers. We did not see her doing any homework, nor did we observe her mother working with her or hear much discussion between the mother and Tracey about her school day. This is very different from what we observed in the other homes. However, the discipline, responsibilities, expectations, quiet, and order were clear. Bronfrenbrenner (1991) points out the importance to educational success of parental supervision of children, high parental expectations of the children, and high educational aspirations. I have observed all of these characteristics in all of the homes of the high achievers, with one exception, and most of these in the homes of the average achievers.

This is not the case, however, for low achievers such as Mycella Falwell, a twelve-year-old seventh grader who attends the same middle school as six of the twelve students observed. Mycella received C's, D's, and F's for her last two academic terms. She lives with her grandmother, who has lived in the same house for twenty years. Mycella expects to attend college but said that "it is so hard to pass science" and that her problems with both science and Spanish stand in her way. She indicated that she receives no help from her grandmother with her schoolwork.

During the first visit to the Falwell home, Mycella was joined by her friends Stephanie Adams, one of the high achievers in the study, and Jesse. They moved to Mycella's bedroom because she had been asked by her grandmother to clean that room, which was a mess, according to the observer. She did not clean the room. The girls discussed an upcoming dance and different hairstyles and then moved on to listening to rap music on a CD player. During this time school was never mentioned, and Ms. Black, the grandmother, never asked Mycella about her school day.

The next visit took place on another weekday, and again Mycella was joined by Stephanie. They sat in Mycella's sister's room tuned into a chat room on the Internet. This time Ms. Black came to the room and asked Mycella about her homework. Mycella told her that she was finished with the work. This was not true, however; she had previously told Stephanie that she had forgotten her math textbook and was unable to complete the assignment. Ms. Black made no effort to look at the work, and Mycella apparently felt comfortable being untruthful to her grandmother.

Later that evening, Stephanie pointed out that Mycella had been asked to leave various classes, apparently for disciplinary reasons. During the next visit Stephanie was arriving as the observer got to the door, and Jesse was there as well. All three girls went to Mycella's sister's room to work on her computer; Jesse did her science homework, while Stephanie completed Mycella's assignment for her. Mycella mentioned that she was failing two classes but didn't seem particularly bothered by this. The observer, who did not know that Stephanie is an outstanding student, noted that Stephanie appeared to be the best student of the three and Mycella the least concerned with school or her performance.

Mycella's life is not centered around her schoolwork, or her extracurricular activities, or her household responsibilities, as is the case for most of the average achievers and almost all of the high achievers. She seems to center her life around her friends. We did observe her at a choir meeting at Family Focus one evening, but even there she seemed disinterested, and did not even note the dates and times of the upcoming concerts. When the observer and Mycella arrived at Mycella's house, Ms. Black would not allow the observer to enter Mycella's bedroom because she said that it was too messy, even though Mycella had been told to clean it earlier. Mycella did not seem to have the same concern for order or discipline that we saw in Pierre or Stephanie or Marie. During another visit to Mycella's home, she and her older sister argued over the use of the computer in the sister's room. Mycella wanted to check her messages on the Internet, and her sister wanted to do homework. Mycella won out. Indeed, Mycella almost never did her homework during the weeks that we observed her. She is not particularly disciplined or responsible, nor does she seem very much interested in education.

Then there is Camille Dunn. Camille is a fifteen-year-old high school freshman. Her grades were mostly C's and D's, though she said that education is "very important" to her. Her mother has lived in Evanston for twenty-five of her thirty-five years; her father is a maintenance worker. Both of her parents graduated from high school, and her mother believes that Camille's education is "very important" and would like to see her graduate from college and to "be somebody." Ms. Dunn indicated that she helps Camille with her homework and encourages her to assert herself.

Camille herself indicated that she is doing well in school, despite the low grades, and said that she needs to have an education. Either she has a hazy idea about student performance, or she believes that her low grades are acceptable.

During our first visit to the Dunn household the observer noticed evidence of possible drug use in the house. Clearly, if this is the case, her parents may not be in position to be as supportive, encouraging, or nurturing as they need to be if Camille is to be properly prepared for school. During the next visit Camille left home and went to Family Focus, which is very close to her home, and entered a homework room in which students whose parents may not be home from work do their homework after school. Camille did no homework but laughed and joked with other girls the entire time.

In fact, Camille never was seen doing homework by the observer during the numerous visits with her. Almost never was dinner served; Camille often stopped at a local grocery for treats. Ms. Dunn was rarely at home during our observations, leaving the observer with Camille and her sister. During one visit both Ms. and Mr. Dunn were at home, and Ms. Dunn prepared dinner. The observer pointed out that this was the only time Ms. Dunn performed "any type of motherly or wifely activity." Even this time, Camille and her sister left and went to Family Focus, though they did no schoolwork, focusing instead on listening to rap music.

When Camille and her sister left Family Focus, they joined a group of young people on a corner. A number of the members of this group passed around what appeared to be a marijuana cigarette. A bit later the Dunns left the group and headed home, just as several cars pulled up to the group, and money and drugs appeared to be exchanged. Camille entered the lobby of her apartment building only to reemerge minutes later and move again toward the group on the corner. When someone yelled "Scatter" and a police car pulled up, the group dispersed.

During our observation Camille never did any household chores, never did any homework, never interacted with her parents in any meaningful way, never was involved in learning or extracurricular activities. Her parents were never seen supporting or encouraging her. Her mother drank beer while the girls prepared dinner on two occasions. For the most part, Camille raises herself.

Clearly, this is not the picture of the family in which a student is being properly prepared for the educational experience. It is also not the picture we have seen with any of the poor Latino families studied. On the other hand, the homes of the poor Latino students are in some significant ways more like those of the lower-achieving black students than those of the better black students.

Eloise Ceja does not think that her education is important and does not care about school. In fact, she said she only wants to complete part of high school, compared to the better black students who all want a postcollege education. She devotes half an hour a day to schoolwork compared to the two to four hours on the part of the higher-achieving black students. Most of the poor black higher achievers indicated that their families were most important in their lives, while Eloise said that "nothing" was important to her.

But Natalie, Eloise's younger sister, is very different. Her education is important to her, and we did see her doing her schoolwork. The Cejas seem to watch the television quite a bit. In the homes of the better black students, the television is generally off, or only the parents watch it.

While Ms. Ceja indicated that she wished that there were more after-school activities for her children, the reality is that there are many such activities, and they are for the most part free. The better black students, like Stephanie Adams, manage to involve themselves in these activities. It is almost as though Ms. Ceja understands the value of these activities but does not understand how the educational system works to fit these activities into a student's life. Ms. Ceja requires discipline and responsibility of her children, though Eloise seems to miss these points. However, the type of structure and order in the home that centers around the school activities of the children is simply not consistently there.

When Ms. Adams returns home from work, she wants to know whether each child has performed their home responsibilities, said their prayers, and exactly what their educational day was like. We do not see this type of structure or attention to education in the Ceja home. When Fermi Adams, the preschooler, showed his mother his drawings, she called him "the smartest boy in the world," clearly an attempt to raise his self-esteem. When seven-year-old Devin Ceja properly determined the number of hot dogs needed to feed the family, his mother also congratulated him. Both mothers encouraged the youngsters to think and to perform well, and both worked on their self-esteem. Both of the older Ceja girls do some household chores, but both seem to spend a lot of time in the yard playing too.

Ms. Ceja worked with Devin on his math, and she told Devin that he could not watch television until he had completed his math homework, occasionally working with him. The problem, of course, is that she speaks only Spanish, and she is limited in what she can do to help, though the actual help is not as important as the gesture.

Like most of the Latino mothers observed, Ms. Ceja has no job outside of the home. This gives her the time, and perhaps the energy, to devote to the home and to the proper preparation of her children that few of the poor black mothers have, given that almost all of them work full-time. But her actions and words with the children, while generally positive and helpful, are not consistent or well structured. She is not Ms. Adams, but she is not Ms. Dunn. If anything, she seems to want to do what is best for her children, but she does not seem to know what that is, or how to do it. More and more, I think that the lack of experience with the American educational system is a real limitation, but it can be overcome with the proper training, I suspect.

When Ms. Maradiaga told her two sons to turn the computer off, Randy replied, "That sucks" and "Shit." Ms. Maradiaga said nothing. When Pierre Baroque wanted his brother to be quiet so that he could work on his schoolwork and said to him, "ffff," his mother quickly said, "Don't say whatever you are about to say." When he said that he was only going to say "freak," she sternly told him that he could not say that either. Randy Maradiaga went to bathe rather than begin his homework as his mother had instructed. When the middle Adams boy was told by his mother to "clean the bathroom. If it isn't clean, I'll use your head to clean the inside of the toilet," Babe quickly complied. Again, Ms. Maradiaga wants the quiet necessary for a sound learning environment, and she wants the children to learn discipline and to pay attention to their learning, but she doesn't seem to know what to do to bring this about. A number of the poor black mothers know, so we cannot say that this is a poverty issue.

Ms. Gomez has been in Evanston for thirteen years, yet she speaks no English, meaning that her ability to help Jose, the second grader, with his work is limited, and this may well limit her efforts to try. She plays with puzzles and cubes with her three-year-old and one-year-old daughters, activities that help them with shapes and colors, with all of the conversation in Spanish. When one of the daughters gave the correct answers to her questions about colors, she applauded her, just as Ms. Adams did her son. She is clearly concerned about, and tried to build, her children's self-esteem.

But neither she nor her husband asked Jose about his school day or his schoolwork, and Jose seems to spend a lot of time playing and watching television even on school days. This is not what the poor black high or average achievers do. She had Jose wash his own clothes one day because he had come home covered in mud. So, she is teaching him responsibility, and when he did not do the job to her satisfaction, she had him do it again. He is learning discipline as well.

In the homes of the average and high-achieving blacks, discipline, responsibility, quiet, and education seem to be almost sacred. Education is discussed daily. Responsibilities are carried out daily. Discipline is stressed daily. The students regularly engage in extracurricular activities. The students devote two to four hours a day to schoolwork, and their mothers make certain that they do so.

In the Galindo home the television is on almost all of the time, and Danny will not complete his homework unless Ms. Galindo makes certain that he does so. At least she is aware of this and realizes what she needs to do. The problem is that she does not do it every day, nor does she do anything to try to get Danny to the point where this is not necessary. It is not necessary in the Thomas or the Adams homes. The Galindo children watch the television a lot, and at one point Eriberto told the observer that he did not know when he would do his homework, perhaps later, while he watched television.

Some of the differences between the black and Latino families may be due to the difference in age among the students observed. All but one of the twelve black students observed were in middle school or were freshmen in high school, while only two of the twenty-one Latino children were this old. Still, twelve of the Latino children were in school and need to be properly prepared for that experience. Younger students are indeed expected to play more than their older counterparts, but the parents need to create an environment that facilitates learning, self-control, responsibility, positive self-esteem, order, structure, and discipline. While play is certainly to be a part of this process for younger children, parents need to help shape this activity to serve the desired goals. I saw this to some extent in the Latino households, but not as often as should be the case, and not as often as we might like.

I am reasonably comfortable with the argument that some of the difference in the preparation by a number of the poor black households in which the children do well in school and the poor Latino households that do not seem to consistently do the things or have the attitudes that I saw in these black households is a function of the black parents' experience with the American educational system. However, the parents of Stephanie Adams, a high achiever, and Tracey Love, an average student, migrated to the United States from Africa and the Bahamas, respectively. In fact, they have been in Evanston for fewer years than a number of the Latino parents. I think that this idea needs more examination.

All of the Latino mothers appear to be very attentive to, and concerned with, their children, monitoring their whereabouts frequently and showing concern about their selection of friends and playmates. In some instances, they manage to translate these concerns and this attentiveness into actions and words that will help prepare their children for the educational experience. In others, they seem almost oblivious to what is needed. They lack the consistency and rigor of, say, a Ms. Adams or a Ms. Baroque. When Mary Rangel asked her mother to read to her, she did not because she had just started to cook. It seems that nothing, including the fact that the black mothers work full-time, stops them from serious involvement in their children's educational activities.

Ms. Rangel takes Mary to swimming classes and teaches her to be respectful and inclusive, in addition to teaching her to delay gratification. So, in several ways she is preparing Mary well for school, while in others, she is lacking. This was often the case for the average-achieving black students.

Peregoy and Boyle (1993) suggest that classroom teachers should be aware of a number of cultural variables that may affect learning and, therefore,

teaching. These include: family structure, roles and interpersonal relationships, discipline, time and space, health and hygiene, and history, traditions,
and holidays, among other variables. They raise questions such as, what does
discipline mean? how important is punctuality? and what is the hierarchy of
authority in the household? According to Grant (1995), these are important
questions about cultures that help teachers to "analyze the level of cultural
congruence in the patterning of teacher-pupil interaction, identify cross-
cultural similarities and differences, and utilize aspects of culture to help children achieve" (p. 12).

Apparently Grant (1995) believes that Latinos may have notions of time
and space, discipline, and rites of passage, among others, that are cultural and
influence their learning and therefore their preparation for learning. What appear to be differences between some poor blacks and poor Latinos may well
be cultural, and some, like Grant (1995) and Grossman (1995), seem to believe that school systems should change or adapt to deal with these differences. As I have written, I am not convinced that the picture is really so clear.
I am simply not convinced that there is one Latino culture simply because
most Latinos speak one language.

Puerto Rico is not Mexico, Mexico is not Bolivia, and Boliva is not Cuba.
Given that almost all of the parents we observed are from Mexico, it is indeed
possible, perhaps likely, that there are Mexican cultural differences at work
here. But the Rangels have been in Evanston for nine years. The Gomez family has been in Evanston for thirteen years. How long does it take to "adapt"?
How long does it take to learn the language in which your children are
taught? Should they have to adapt, or should the school system adapt to
them?

George I. Sanchez (1997) seems to suggest some sort of combination,
with most of the responsibility on the family, when he writes: "There are
many thousands of persons in the Southwest whose mother tongue was
Spanish, who were socially and economically disadvantaged (that is, who
were in the same environment situation as that of the Spanish-speaking
children who fail miserably in many public schools today), and who did
'make the grade.' To attribute this to the suggestion that 'they were different' does not accord with statistics on the distribution of intelligence." He
goes on to suggest that the difference is the quality of the schools.
He writes, "Good schools—and by this we do not mean anything extraor-

dinary, just good schools as judged the country over, take the 'problem' of the Spanish-speaking child in stride" (p. 132).

Sanchez, who died in 1972, was considered "the pioneer in bilingual/bicultural education" (Darder, Torres, and Gutierrez 1997, 488). He does not seem to argue that the schools need to turn themselves upside down in order to adapt, even to the obvious language difference, let alone the less obvious cultural differences. Poor Latinos can and do perform well in school. I believe that the key is that those who do well are middle class in their values, beliefs, and attitudes. This should come as no surprise given that public schools are middle class in their organization, structure, and expected "output."

The Chapa family is one such middle-class, and middle-income, family. Ms. Chapa insists that six-year-old Anthony follow a daily schedule that centers around his homework, and he watches only one television show a day. When he and his brother disagree, she scolds them and punishes Anthony. She helps Anthony with his homework daily, and on one occasion told him that he could not go to the park if he did not quiet down. Jesus Maradiaga, a ten-year-old, told his cousin Jose that he would get up and "kick [his] butt" if he did not quiet down. This kind of behavior and language just would not happen in the Chapa household, or the Adams household, or the Baroque household.

Mr. Perez, like Mr. Ceja, is more involved in the upbringing of his children than any of the black fathers. The Latinos may well sacrifice an income for the wife so that she can raise the children, suggesting that a very high priority is placed upon their proper upbringing and development. Yet, a number of the parents fail to do these things as consistently as do the parents of other poor, academically successful students. This may also suggest a difference between the poor blacks and the poor Latinos in terms of roles. In Latino families, it may be that the mother is supposed to be the caretaker and nurturer and the father the breadwinner, the authority figure. This could work to the advantage of the children, although it does not always do so.

Overall, the greatest differences that I see between the Latino families and the black families in terms of preparing their children for school involve the consistency and the rigor with which the parents of the average and high-achieving black students involve themselves in the academic lives of their children. In most of the Latino families a number of the ingredients for success are in place, unlike the cases of the black families in which the children do poorly.

Now how do we translate these ingredients into the appropriate actions, beliefs, and attitudes?

6

POLICY IMPLICATIONS: SO, NOW WHAT?

Let me again point out that I agree with Hurst (1996) that the family offers the greatest opportunity for educational improvement. I do not believe that longer school days, more school hours, student uniforms, more tests, vouchers, privatization, decentralization, centralization, more-stringent requirements for teachers (in the midst of a massive teacher shortage in many areas) offer us much hope for significantly improving the education offered to poor, nonwhite students in urban areas. Neither do I think that simply having parents come to more school functions is the answer, though parents who come to school are more likely to be the same parents who do and say the right things at home.

I do not believe that the types of policy changes currently being explored around the nation hold much promise for significant, long-term improvements in the education offered to poor, urban, nonwhite students. I agree with Comer (1993) that public schools are in fact middle-class institutions, and, as such, they work best for middle-class students, regardless of the income level of these students. Middle-income students perform better than others in public schools, not because they are more intelligent than others, but because they possess the characteristics, beliefs, and attitudes prized by schools.

They have the discipline to sit still all day even when the subject is boring. Rather than rush outside to play on a warm spring day, they concentrate in class because they know that in the future this effort will pay off. They have high enough self-esteem that they do not fall apart when criticized by a teacher. They know how to work in groups because they have learned to co-operate. They accept the responsibility for their own actions and perfor-mance because they know how to accept responsibility and because they are internally controlled. Are they born with these characteristics? Of course not! They learn them, and if they learn them early and often at home, they have an advantage when it comes to school, the environment that requires these characteristics if students are to do well.

It is clear both from the current research and my earlier work (Sampson 2002) that poor urban nonwhites can and do possess many of these charac-teristics and perform well in school as a result. Not all of them do, but not all do not, either. Those who do and perform well in school are not "different," nor are they "white" or "Anglo." They are poor folks whose parents some-how seem to understand not only the value of their children's education but also just what they must do to properly prepare them for this education. They are middle-class poor people.

This of course suggests that I am defining social class by means other than the traditional variables of education, occupation, and income (Samp-son 1973). While these variables may well be useful in discussions of social class, it seems to me that more important than how much folks earn, or how much education they have, or the rank of their jobs on an occupational pres-tige scale is how they act, what they value, or what they believe as a result of these more easily measurable characteristics. While it is much easier to mea-sure income and education than self-esteem or discipline, I believe that it is the latter set of variables that is more important, both because the real issue is what impact do the income, education, and occupation have on attitudes and behavior and because it appears that behavior and attitudes are not com-pletely tied to variables such as education, occupation, and income. Nor are they tied completely to race or ethnicity.

Edward Banfield (1970) indicated that the middle class is oriented to-ward the future, high in self-esteem, internally controlled, and independent. He saw the lower class as low in self-esteem, apathetic, and externally con-trolled. Oscar Lewis (1966) also saw the lower class—and he meant lower in-come when he referred to the lower class—as fatalistic, low in self-esteem (a "weak ego structure"), lacking the ability to delay gratification, and exter-nally controlled. A number of scholars, including Frazier (1957), Lewis

(1966), Glazer and Moynihan (1963), and Mead (1986), attribute these characteristics to those with lower incomes, little education, and lower-ranked occupations—the lower class.

I disagree with this characterization. Eight of the poor black families that I observed (Sampson 2002) and most of the eight poor Latino families observed for this research showed few of these characteristics, and some showed none of them. To be sure, I saw many of them among the poor black families in which the children do poorly in school but not among the average or high achievers, and I saw a number of the characteristics that these scholars and others would attribute to the middle class.

Middle-class parents tend to properly prepare their children for the educational experience not because they have more money or greater intelligence, but because they have the values, attitudes, and beliefs upon which that experience is based. Some poor parents apparently also have them, and that includes poor blacks and poor Latinos. Again, however, the poor Latinos whom I studied did not show these traits as consistently or as rigorously as did the poor black parents of the higher-achieving students. On the other hand, they were nothing like the parents of the lower-achieving black students, either.

Valentine (1968), Glazer and Moynihan (1963), and Frazier (1957) see these characteristics as cultural, that is, as handed down from generation to generation. I see them less as cultural and more as adaptive. Many people when faced with consistent poverty naturally adapt to those conditions, but many do not and aim to get to a different place, or at least to help their children get there. But even if they are cultural, it would be, as Valentine refers to it, a "culture of poverty" and not the culture of blacks or of Latinos. Many folks in poverty whom I have observed have virtually none of the characteristics ascribed to this culture of poverty, so one must wonder about the accuracy of this characterization.

It is very difficult for those in poverty and living in poor neighborhoods to maintain the values, beliefs, attitudes, and behavior that I consider middle class and that are necessary if the children are to do well in school. Believing in a future is not easy when many around you are standing on the corner selling drugs or their bodies, or drinking beer, or unemployed. It is hard when many around you have no future, and their lives are not really in their hands but in the hands of the police or the addiction or the probation officer or the unemployment office. When young people grow up in neighborhoods in which no one goes off to work every day, discipline and responsibility are not easy to teach.

Yet, these and other important lessons are taught every day to many poor children by their parents, most often the mother. Some of the poor apparently do not have enough of the required characteristics, and for the most part I suspect that their children will do poorly. Comer (1993) writes, "The experience of children who grow up in social networks that are marginal to the mainstream of society is often quite different, more likely to produce social and academic failure in school" (306). By "mainstream" he means "middle class."

I am not going to debate here whether there is a culture of poverty or basic differences between the poor and the nonpoor. There are clearly middle-class poor people doing the right things to maximize the possibility that their children will do well in school, and there are others who are not. Why not? is a question beyond my data.

If we know that the family has the capacity to make this magnitude of difference in how children do in school, what do we do about it, and why haven't we been doing what needs to be done? If we know that poor mothers such as Ms. Baroque, Ms. Love, Ms. Perez, and Ms. Rangel not only care very much about the education of their children but also seem to know what to do to translate this care into actions and results and that others do not (e.g., Ms. Dunn), what are we doing to help those who do not? Can we teach or help others to emulate the Adams family or the Chapa family?

Laurence Steinberg (1998) is certainly correct when he asserts, "A sizable part of the variability in student performance is determined by factors outside of school" (p. 322). Furthermore, "Education reformers have, for the most part, been guilty of a sort of myopia that has zeroed in on schools and classrooms and has paid only passing attention to the broader context in which schools and classrooms function." Policy makers and politicians focus on schools because they have some control over them. They can change school administrations, teacher requirements, dress codes, length of the school day and year, funding arrangements, and admission requirements. Indeed, all of these have changed, and still the education of poor urban non-whites has not significantly improved.

How many more generations of these youngsters will we experiment with before we become serious, dedicated, and thoughtful enough to make serious changes? I do not consider myself a change maker. I am a scholar. However, I have watched too long while class after class of poor, urban nonwhite students fail to receive the education they deserve and need, and group after group of policy makers, educators, and politicians fails to respond properly. After this research and my earlier work (Sampson 2002), I am convinced that there are enough examples among the poor, both Latinos and black, of families trying to do the right things that we can learn valuable lessons from them and put these lessons to use. Again, I caution that the poor Latinos may well present an issue not seen among blacks—language— that might have to be addressed.

Most often when we discuss parents and schools, we talk about getting parents to attend more school functions. On one hand, this makes sense, because the more parents are at school, the more likely it is that they will gain more knowledge about schools and education that might help them better prepare their children. On the other hand, teachers are educated. They dress a certain way, talk a certain way, drive certain cars. They take vacations in nice places. Poor folks have none of this, and these differences may make them uncomfortable in the school setting.

When the poor black mothers I observed come home from work, they must ask about the school day, help with homework, monitor the chores, discuss the extracurricular activities—all before dinner. With one exception, the poor Latino mothers I observed do not work, but they all have young children who require a great deal of attention and energy, and for the most part they do not speak the same language as the teachers. These women, who, with a few notable exceptions, clearly bear almost all of the responsibility for the care of the children, it seems to me would be either too tired, too stressed, too embarrassed, or too intimidated to be much involved with the school. Still, some try.

Parental involvement needs to be seen as active involvement in preparing their children for school and not simply attending a PTA meeting or conference. This may involve working with families, and this is not easy, but it is infinitely better than the alternatives. The Chicago public schools, for example, in attempts to improve the education for their student population, which is about 85 percent minority (mostly blacks and Latinos), have tried decentralization of decision making, centralization of decision making, and charter schools and are now high on a longer school day. This latest development comes as a result of a front-page story in the *Chicago Tribune* that relates higher pupil performance on standardized tests to a longer school day.

The article states, "Poor-performing districts tend to have shorter school days. Those are also the districts with higher-than-average concentrations of poor and minority students. Wealthier districts with better tests scores tend to have longer school days." It goes on to say that the head of the public schools and the head of the local teachers union, after hearing of the paper's "findings," want to "discuss" a longer school day and lobby the state legislature for the money to bring this about (Rado 2002). This is nonsense of the highest order. The time in school is not the issue. Wealthier districts have middle-class parents who properly prepare their children for school, which allows students in those districts to perform better on the tests. It is not even the money spent on the schools that is the key. It is what the parents of the school children do and do not do.

The article goes on to say that "some experts believe low test scores may have more to do with student poverty than a short school day" (Rado 2002). They are right and wrong. Poverty is a key, but it does not stop the young Perez boy or Stephanie Adams. Again, it is not poverty per se but the higher probability among the poor that parents will not or cannot properly prepare their children for the educational experience.

I mention this example both because Chicago sees itself as a leader among urban school districts and because it is a prime example of policy makers rushing to implement a policy that has little chance of success because they have no real idea of what else to do and because they have some control over the school day. They act even in the absence of research that clearly shows that this new direction can help significantly. Such research would have to control not only for the income of the people in the school district but also for the attitudes, values, and beliefs of the parents in the district—that is, the parents' social class.

The article itself points out that the link is not between length of the school day and achievement, but wealth and achievement. Though the author does not seem to understand that link or self-selection, she does pay it passing attention. Middle-class, middle-income parents tend to live in districts that have more money to spend on schools. And longer school days. However, it is not the money but the preparation for school that is more important. A longer school day is not the issue, but it tends to go along with the money.

The article even mentions the high school district in Evanston as a high-performing district with a longer school day and money to spend on a variety of instructional options. It did not look at Camille Dunn, who, I suspect, could stay in class for hours on end and do no better, because she doesn't care, she doesn't want to, she doesn't see the value in it; her parents do nothing to change this and apparently have done little to point her in the right direction. So more poor nonwhite students will suffer while they wait for a policy maker with the insight, the knowledge, and the courage to move in the right direction.

Moving in this direction is, however, not at all easy. As Furstenberg et al. (1999) correctly state, "Americans strongly adhere to the ideal of a family system protected from government interference, in which children's fates are almost entirely in the hands of parents" (p. 226). In other words, we really do not want to seriously involve other institutions in the operation of families in this country. While I understand the motivations for this position, I also understand that many poor urban nonwhite students continue to do poorly in school and continue, as a result, to have very little chance at a successful, productive future in our country. This research suggests that in the case of poor Latinos, some family intervention may be helpful.

Clark (1983), writing about poor black families, states, "Perhaps we can identify certain problem areas that need to be addressed in individual families" (p. 200). On his list of the characteristics of high-achieving poor students are several that I have observed in a number of the Latino homes studied for this work. A number, however, are missing from these homes, such as frequent parent-initiated contact with schools, the expectation by the parents that they will play a major role in their children's education, parental expectation that their children will receive postsecondary education, interaction among siblings as organized subgroups, parents' frequent engagement in achievement-training activities, and specific parental achievement-oriented norms and rules for the children.

I observed that for the most part the parents are emotionally calm with the children and do monitor the children frequently, but the "rules" enforcement is haphazard at best. The parents provide some nurturance and support, though not as much as perhaps should be provided in some of the homes. Should society intervene with these families to help them get to the point where they can consistently provide the guidance, training, and direction that we see among higher-achieving poor nonwhite students? If society should intervene, just how should this be done?

Clark's list of the characteristics of the higher achievers is not very different from the characteristics that I have found to correlate with high achievement among poor blacks, though his list may be a bit more specific. I stress discipline, cooperation, internal control, high educational aspirations, a future orientation, delayed gratification, a sense of responsibility, and an orderly, structured, and quiet home environment. These are characteristics that would seem to form the basis for those identified by Clark, and I believe they should be the goals for most families.

Fortunately, several of them are in place in a number of the Latino families that I observed, but others are not, especially the high educational aspirations, the future orientation, and the home environment. A number of the parents are simply not very much involved in the education of their children. This may well be the result of the inability of most of the parents to speak English and their lack of familiarity with the American educational system.

Race, poverty, and language are certainly obstacles to receiving a quality education. They are, however, not absolute obstacles. Some poor Latino parents, such as Ms. Galindo and Ms. Perez, seem to overcome such obstacles quite well and to do most of the things required to prepare their children for school. Ms. Perez speaks English, and Ms. Galindo takes an English class, which may in fact mean that language is not really an obstacle for them. While Ms. Chapa does not speak English, her husband does, and for them poverty is not an issue. They are almost a textbook case of how to properly prepare children for school, but they are also middle income and well educated, clearly middle-class people.

The issue, then, is clear for me: What do we do to help the families that do not or cannot consistently do the things necessary to send the child to school prepared to learn? How do we get the Maradiagas to be more like the Perezes, or the Cejas more like the Chapas or the Galindos? We cannot give them the Chapas' money or education or experiences, but the Galindos have none of these and they manage to do much of what Eriberto, Danny, and Ana need to do well in school. Schools alone cannot bring about these changes, and unless and until these changes take place, many poor non-white students will fail to benefit from the education offered them, not because they want to fail, but because they are not adequately prepared for the education.

I do not mean to suggest that schools are not important here. They certainly are. If schools lack dedicated and concerned teachers or the necessary resources or space, they may well not be in a position to properly teach students. Small class size—fifteen to twenty students per class—has a positive impact on student performance, as does preschool education. It is unlikely that many urban school systems with large numbers of poor students will have the resources, or perhaps the political will, to cut class sizes to this level or to implement preschool education for all youngsters and to sustain it long enough.

If parents are not sending their children to school prepared to learn, if they are low in self-esteem, or are noncooperative or lack discipline or are present oriented or have low educational aspirations, then what schools can do is quite limited. Schools can do a lot, but the family offers the greatest opportunity for improvements in education, in my view. This suggests some sort of family-intervention approach. It may be that community-based agencies such as Family Focus, which seems to have the trust of many poor Latino families, can work with willing families to help them fashion the desired home environment and teach them the importance of regularly working with the children on their schoolwork, building their children's self-esteem, and requiring discipline, responsibility, and cooperation.

In the case of the poor Latinos it may well be necessary to teach the parents more about the American educational system, so that they have a better idea of the value of the changes they are being asked to make. Given that a number of the parents interviewed indicated that the primary reason that they moved from Mexico was to allow their children the opportunity to receive a better education, many may already be sufficiently motivated to be open to this type of intervention. Because many poor folks do not trust outsiders (Clark 1983; Furstenberg et al. 1999), it is not easy to go into their homes, especially if the purpose is to let them know that they need to change to become more effective parents.

Perhaps this could be done within the context of support groups, especially if Grossman (1995) is correct in his assessment that Latinos prefer to work in groups. Rather than sending trained parental educators into homes, it may be best to have parents work with trainers in groups. Of course, the trainers must observe the families enough to know what each family needs.

We talk a lot about the family in America, but we are understandably reluctant to do much about it. This needs to change if we really want significant improvement in the education offered to, and received by, poor nonwhite students. This kind of effort takes a great deal of time. We are not talking about teaching new mothers how to change diapers. We are talking about teaching parents how to use extracurricular activities and household chores to help teach responsibility, discipline, and heightened self-esteem. We are talking about teaching them why it is necessary to read consistently to preschoolers and teach them to delay gratification. We are talking about teaching parents the value to their children's education of a quiet, orderly, and structured home environment, an environment that is to some degree centered around their children's learning.

If Grossman (1995) is correct in his argument about the importance of the family to Latinos, they may be more amenable to efforts to improve the education of family members—or they may well be less open to intervention in family life. These are not simple issues to address, but to fail to try risks, in my view, a continuation of high drop-out rates, low test scores, and generally poor school performances.

I am suggesting that we try to teach some non-middle-class Latino families to act more middle class in the ways in which they deal with their children. This is not asking them to become more "Anglo," for whites have no monopoly on middle-class values, attitudes, or beliefs. As long as public schools remain middle-class institutions, the children of the middle class will have an advantage and will continue to do better than others. If the "others" want their children to perform better, they will have to become more aware of just what those middle-class attitudes, beliefs, and values are and how their behavior can influence development of these attitudes in their children.

My research suggests that in most of the Latino homes there is a base upon which we can build. This was not really the case for the poor black homes I studied in which the students performed poorly in school. In these homes, I saw almost none of the characteristics of the homes of successful students.

I am, however, again drawn back to the argument over language. While I see the inability of most of the parents observed to speak English as hindering their efforts to prepare their children well for school, others disagree. In fact, there are those such as Kjolseth (1982) and Garcia (1991) who believe it is important for Latinos to maintain the language difference for either cultural reasons (Garcia) or power reasons (Ruiz 1997). Kjolseth (1982) writes, "Chicano families who desire the maintenance of the ethnic language *must* exercise their control over that single domain of language use where they do have effective and continuing control: the family. Parental insistence upon the use of Spanish by themselves and their children within the private family domain is the *only* realistic hope" (p. 25). While this makes sense to me, I wonder how this affects the children's use of English.

I would not argue at all that Latinos who speak Spanish need to learn to speak English as their only language or teach their children to use it as their only language. My point is that the inability to speak English limits what the parents can do in schools for their children as long as those schools continue to operate only in English; it also limits what they can do outside of schools that might be beneficial to their children. I am a supporter of speaking both languages, but my observations suggest that speaking only one of them can be limiting.

So, I am not suggesting that the parents who seem to need help need to speak English. I believe that they need to understand what the American educational system values, what it is really like, what it requires, and what they need to do to prepare their children for that system. Whether they learn these lessons in English or Spanish is not the point, though it is still difficult to know whether to sign a permission slip for participation in a sport or musical group or a class trip if the slip is in English and the parent speaks no English. It is difficult to talk to a second grader about her schoolwork if the worksheets are in English and the parent speaks only Spanish.

Whether the lack of English-speaking ability is more important than the lack of experience with the American educational system, I do not know. My data do not allow me to determine this. I see them both as issues, but it is true that all of the poor black families that I have studied (Sampson 2002) and that Clark (1983), Furstenberg et al. (1999), and Bempechat (1998) studied speak English, and still some of them do few of the things needed by their children. Teaching parents to help children learn the importance of delaying gratification, or the value of discipline, or internal control, or responsibility, or high self-esteem can be done in any language. Helping with homework that is written in English cannot, nor can understanding messages from school that are written in English. It would be difficult for a parent to feel comfortable at a child's school play if everyone else spoke English. So, I believe that the language barrier is an issue but not necessarily one to be solved by asking Latinos to give up one language for another.

The staff of community-based agencies such as Family Focus could be very helpful in identifying those characteristics, values, and attitudes in families that need to be changed in order to better prepare children for school. These staff members would have to be trained to know these necessary values and characteristics, to identify them in homes and families, and to teach them to those who need them. This process is invasive and time consuming, but it has promise, I believe. The schools need to be partners in this process as well. They need to be aware of, and sensitive to, parents' efforts to improve their child-preparation skills.

I suspect that some families will not want to be bothered and others will need other types of assistance before we can proceed to the kind of skills about which I am writing. Parents who have drug or alcohol problems, for example, will probably need to address these before we can move to parenting skills. Unless these problems are addressed, parenting skills mean very little.

Many urban neighborhoods have changed such that ghettos and barrios have become slums, as middle-class residents, who could serve as role models for others, have fled to safer, more acceptable areas, leaving behind only the poor to learn from each other. As a result, those desired values, attitudes, and behaviors are in short supply. Without these folks to serve as models, many poor folks have not learned what it takes to do well in school and in life. It is not that they cannot learn, for, obviously, many not only have learned but are successful in using that knowledge to properly prepare their children for school and for life. Why some poor Latinos seem to know much of what to do while others seem to know or to do much less is beyond my data to answer.

We need to observe many more poor Latino families, including those who come from places other than Mexico, if we are to gain more insight into the family dynamics and patterns that affect the preparation of their children for school. Eight families is only the start, and families from other countries might help us get a better handle on the role of culture.

A larger group might also allow investigation into the influence of the length of time spent in the United States on school preparation. It may well be that those who have been here longer and therefore may have a better sense of the requirements of the American educational system do more of the desired things than do others. A larger sample would be required for this determination.

Finally, we know what parents need to do to help prepare both preschoolers and school-age children for the school experience. We have learned that many poor parents do much of what is needed, even though the school systems and the society seem to improperly lump all poor folks together into a group that either cannot learn or does not want to learn. Poor Latinos are more likely than some poor blacks to do some of the things necessary but less likely than others to do many of them consistently. They appear to lack the knowledge base but not the desire. When will we begin to take advantage of this desire to increase the knowledge base? How much longer can we afford to wait? When will we begin to shift some attention from schools to families? The poor Latino children are waiting.

APPENDIX
INTERVIEW
QUESTIONNAIRES

The interview schedules were used to collect background, attitudinal, and some behavioral data on the families and students. The observers asked the questions whenever both they and the parents and students felt comfortable. In all of the cases the interviews with the parents were done in Spanish, given that few of them spoke any English. In some cases the student interviews were done in English, and in a few, in Spanish. As a result, I have included both the English and the Spanish versions of the questionnaires.

PARENTAL QUESTIONNAIRE

DePaul University

Hello, I am _____, from DePaul University. We are, as you know, studying how parents or guardians in Evanston relate to their children. I would like to conduct a short interview with the person responsible for the children in this household. May I talk to that person?

(Once you have been introduced to that person)

I would like to ask you your name, though no real names will be used in the study.

Respondent Name_____

(1) What is your relationship to the children in this house?
   (Probes: Father, Grandfather, Mother, Aunt)

(2) How are you related to the head of the house?
   (Probes: Spouse, Head, Parent, Child)

(3) How long have you lived in Evanston?

(4) In what city or community did you grow up?

(5) How long have you lived in this house?
   (years or months)

(6) How many adults (over 18 years old) including yourself live in this house
   with you?

(7) How many children live here?

(8) How old are you?
   (Age in years at last birthday)

(9) Is the head of the household working or doing something else at present?
   1. Working (Skip to Ques. 10)
   2. Unemployed, but looking for work (Skip to Ques. 12)
   3. Going to school (Skip to Ques. 12)
   4. Retired (Skip to Ques. 13)
   5. Housewife (Skip to Ques. 12)
   6. Unemployed, Not looking for work—This does not include housewife
   (Skip to Ques. 12)

(10) (If employed) What is his/her (your) job?
(Job title, Description)

(11) (If employed) In what type of business does he/she (you) work?
(What does company do?)

(12) (If not working at present) Has the head of the household (you) ever
had a job?
Yes (Skip to Ques. 13)
No (Skip to Ques. 16)
Not Applicable (Skip to Ques. 16)

(13) (If not working at present) How long ago was it that the head of the
household (you) worked?
(Record in months)

(14) (If not working at present) What was the head of the household's (your)
last job?
(Job title, Description)

(15) (If not working at present) In what type of business did he/she (you) work?
(What did company do?)

(16) Are you married or single? (Ask only if not obvious from Ques. 2)
1. Married, includes common law
2. Single
3. Separated or divorced
4. Widowed

(17) (If married) Does your spouse live in the house with you?

(18) (If married) Where is your spouse from? That is, where did he/she
grow up?

(19) (If married, separated, divorced, or widowed) How far did your spouse or ex-spouse go in school?
Grade   Degree

(20) What is the last grade that you completed in school?
Grade   Degree

(21) How important is (Child's name)'s education to you?
(If not important, skip to Ques. 23)

(22) (If at all important) Why is it so important?

(23) If not important, why not?

(24) Do you try to encourage (child's name) to do well in school?

(25) (If yes) How do you encourage him/her?

(26) How many times a year do you visit (child's name)'s school?

(27) How do you feel when you visit the school?
(Probes: Happy, worried, afraid, confident, concerned)

(28) Why do you feel this way?

(29) What, if anything, stands in (child's name)'s way in terms of getting a good education?
(Probes: Health, Teachers, Lack of a future, Money, Family responsibility)

(30) Do other children try to stop (child's name) from doing well in school?
(If no, skip to Ques. 32)

(31) (If yes) How do they do that?

(32) Are there adults at school whom you think try to stop (child's name) from doing well in school?

(33) (If yes) How do they do that?

(34) Do you believe that race and/or discrimination plays a role in your life?
(If yes) How?
(If no, skip to Ques. 35)

(35) Tell me about your upbringing. What was it like?

(36) How do you try to raise (child's name)? (Probes: What is important in raising children? What about discipline? What about self-control? What about the future?)

(37) How many times a week do you read a newspaper?

(38) How many times a week do you read a book?

(39) Upon whom do you rely when you have a problem?

(40) Is there anything else that you wanted to say, or to add?

STUDENT QUESTIONNAIRE

DePaul University

Hello, I am _____ from DePaul University. As you probably already know, we are studying how some families in Evanston get along with their children, and how those children do in school. I would like to conduct a short interview with you about yourself, your family, and school.

I would like to know your name for the record, though no real names will be used in the study, and everything that you say is confidential.

Respondent's name_____

Respondent's gender Male Female

(1) How old were you on your last birthday?
(Age in years)

(2) What grade are you in in school?

(3) What school do you attend?
(Name of school)

(4) What do you like most about the school? (Probes: The teachers? Your teachers? The principal? A specific teacher? The after-school activities? The homework? The students?)

(5) What do like the least about the school?

(6) How well are you doing in school? (Circle one)
1. Very well
2. Well
3. Pretty good/fair
4. Not so well
5. Poorly

(7) How important is education to you? (Circle one)
1. Very important
2. Important
3. Kind of important
4. Not very important
5. Not at all important

(8) Why is this? That is, why is school_____ to you?
(Use the answer from above)

(9) Has any other student ever tried to keep you from doing well in school?
  1. Yes (Go to Question 10)
  2. No (Go to Question 12)

(10) When and how did this happen?

(11) Why do you think that this happened (or happens)?

(12) How much time do you spend on your homework every evening or weekend day?

(13) How far would you like to go in school?

(14) How far do you expect to go in school?

(15) Are there any obstacles in your way? (Circle one answer)
  1. Yes (Go to Ques. 16)
  2. No (Go to Ques. 17)

(16) What are these obstacles?

(17) How many times a week do you read a newspaper?

(18) What is most important to you in your life?

(19) Is there one specific teacher to whom you really feel close, or to whom you used to feel close?
  1. Yes (Go to Quest. 20)
  2. No (Go to Quest. 21)

(20) In what grade was this, and why do/did you feel close?

(21) Is race or racial discrimination something that you think much about? Why or why not?

(22) How much help do you get from your (parent(s)/grandparent/aunt/uncle/whatever is appropriate) with your schoolwork? That is, how often would you say they help you?

(23) Is this enough help for you?
Not enough help?
Too much help?

(24) If you could change one thing about your family life, what would it be?

(25) If you could be one person in the world, who would it be? Why is that?

(27) Is there anything else that you would like to add?

CUESTIONARIO PARA LOS PADRES

Hola. Yo soy _____ de la Universidad de DePaul. Como saben, estamos estudiando como los padres o guardianes en Evanston relacionan con sus hijos. Quisiera conducir un entrevista pequeño con la persona encargada de los niños en este hogar. ¿Puedo hablar con esta persona?
(Después de ser presentado a esa persona)

Quisiera saber su nombre, pero no usamos los nombres verdaderos en el estudio.

Nombre:_____

1. ¿Cómo está usted emparentado a los niños en esta casa? (padre, abuelo, madre, tía, etc.)

2. ¿Cómo está Ud. emparentado al jefe de la casa? (esposo, jefe, madre/padre, hijo)

3. ¿Cuánto tiempo hace que vive Ud. en Evanston?

4. ¿En qué comunidad creció Ud?

5. ¿Cuánto tiempo hace que vive en esta casa?

6. ¿Cuántos adultos (mayor que 18 años), incluyendo a sí mismo, viven en esta casa consigo?

7. ¿Cuántos niños viven aquí?

8. ¿Cuántos años tiene usted? (en años al último cumpleaños)

9. ¿El jefe de la casa trabaja o hace algo diferente hoy en día?
   Trabaja (pase a #10)
   Desempleado, pero buscando trabajo (pase a #12)
   Asiste la escuela (pase a #12)
   Jubilado (pase a #13)
   Ama de casa (pase a #12)
   Desempleado, no buscando trabajo—no incluye la ama de casa (pase a #12)

10. (Si está empleado) ¿Cuál es su trabajo? (título, descripción)

11. (Si está empleado) ¿En qué tipo de nogocios trabaja él/ella/usted? (¿qué hace la compañía?)

12. (No trabaja ahora) ¿Ha tenido trabajo jamás el jefe de la casa?
    Sí (pase a #13)
    No (pase a #16)
    No aplica

13. (No trabaja ahora) ¿Cuánto tiempo hace que el jefe de la casa ha trabajado? (en meses)

14. (No trabaja ahora) ¿Cuál fue su último trabajo? (título y descripción)

15. (No trabaja ahora) ¿En que tipo de negocios trabajó él/ella/usted? (¿qué hizo la compañía?)

16. ¿Está usted casado o soltero? (solamente pregunta esto si no es obvio)
Casado (incluye unión consensual)
Soltero
Separado/Divorciado
Viudo

17. (Si está casado) ¿Vive su esposa en casa consigo?

18. (Si está casado) ¿De dónde es su esposa? ¿Dónde creció ella?

19. (Si está casado, separado, o viudo) ¿A que nivel alcanzó su esposa/ex-esposa en la escuela? (grado) (título)

20. ¿Cuál es el último grado que cumplió usted en la escuela? (grado) (título)

21. ¿Cuánto le importa le educación de (nombre) a usted? (sino le importa, pase a #23)

22. (Si es importante) ¿Por qué sí?

23. (Si no es importante) ¿Por qué no?

24. ¿Trata usted de animar a (nombre) a salir bien en la escuela?
Sí
No

25. (Si responde "sí") ¿Cómo le anima usted?

25. ¿Cuántas veces al año visita usted la escuela de (nombre)?

27. ¿Cómo se siente cuando visita la escuela? (contento, preocupado, asustado, confidente, etc.)

28. ¿Por qué se siente así?

29. ¿Qué cosa impide a (nombre) a recibir una educación buena? (salud, maestros, falta de futuro, dinero, responsabilidad a la familia)

30. ¿Hay otros niños que tratan de impedir el suceso de (nombre) en la escuela? (si las respuesta es "no," pase a #32)

31. (Si responde que sí) ¿Cómo la hacen ellos?

32. ¿Hay adultos en la escuela que en su opinión tratan de impedir a (nombre) a salir bien en la escuela?

33. (Si responde que "sí") ¿Cómo lo hacen ellos?

34. ¿Cree usted que la raza y/o la discriminación tiene papel en su vida? ¿Sí? ¿Cómo?

35. Descríbame su juventud. ¿Cómo era?

36. ¿Cómo trata usted de criar a (nombre)? (¿Cuáles cosas son importantes en criar a los niños? ¿disciplina? ¿auto control? ¿el futuro?)

37. ¿Cuántas veces por semana lee usted el periódico?

38. ¿Cuántas veces por semana lee usted un libro?

39. ¿En quién confía Ud. cuando tiene un problema?

40. ¿Hay algo más que quiere decir o agregar?

CUESTIONARIO PARA LOS ESTUDIANTES

Universidad de De Paul

Hola. Yo soy _____ de la Universidad de De Paul. Como probablemente ya sabes, estudiamos como algunas familias en Evanston se relacionan con sus hijos y como esos hijos salen en la escuela. Quisiera conducir un entrevista breve sobre ti mismo.

Quisiera saber tu nombre para el registro, pero no se usan los nombres verdaderos en el estudio y todo lo que dices se mantiene confidencial.

1. ¿Cuántos años cumpliste en tu último cumpleaños? (en años)

2. ¿En qué grado estás en la escuela?

3. ¿A qué escuela asistes? (nombre de la escuela)

4. ¿Cuál aspecto de la escuela te gusta más? (¿los maestros? ¿tus maestros? ¿el director? ¿un maestro en particular? ¿las actividades después de la escuela? ¿la tarea? ¿los estudiantes?

5. ¿Cuál aspecto de la escuela te gusta menos?

6. ¿Cómo sales en la escuela? (haga círculo)
Muy bien
Bien
Así-así
No muy bien
Mal

7. ¿Cuánto te importa la educación? (haga círculo)
Muy importante
Importante
Bastante importante
No muy importante
Ninguna importancia

8. ¿Por qué? O sea, ¿por qué es la escuela (usa la respuesta de pregunta #7) para ti?

9. ¿Hay otro estudiante que haya tratado de impedir tu éxito en la escuela?
Sí (pasa a #10)
No (pasa a #12)

10. ¿Cuándo? ¿Qué pasó?

11. En tu opinión, ¿por qué paso esto? ¿Por qué pasa en general?

12. ¿Cuánto tiempo pasas con tu tarea cada noche o durante el día los fines de semana?

13. ¿A qué nivel te gustaría alcanzar en la escuela?

14. ¿A qué nivel piensas que alcanzarás en le escuela?

15. ¿Hay obstáculos que te impiden?
    Sí (pasa a #16)
    No (pasa a #17)

16. ¿Cuáles son estos obstáculos?

17. ¿Cuántas veces por semana lees un periódico?

18. ¿Qué te importa más en tu vida?

19. ¿Hay un maestro en particular con quién te sientes muy conectado? ¿Había un maestro particular con quién te sentías muy conectado en el pasado?
    Sí (pasa a #20)
    No (pasa a #21)

20. ¿En qué grado se ocurrió y por qué te sentías tan conectado?

21. ¿Es la raza o la discriminación a causa de la raza algo en que piensas? ¿Por qué sí o por qué no?

22. ¿Cuánta ayuda recibes de tus padres/abuelos/tíos (cualquiera que sea apropiada) con tu tarea? O sea, ¿con qué frecuencia te ayudan?

23. ¿Es suficiente? ¿No es suficiente? ¿Es demasiado?

24. Si pudieras cambiar una cosa de tu vida familiar, ¿qué sería?

25. Si pudieras ser cualquiera persona del mundo, ¿quién sería? ¿Por qué?

26. ¿Hay algo más que te gustaría decir o agregar?

REFERENCES

WORKS CITED

Banfield, E. 1970. *The Unheavenly City.* Boston: Little, Brown.

Bempechat, J. 1998. *Against the Odds: How At-Risk Children Exceed Expectations.* San Francisco: Jossey-Bass.

Berliner, D. C., and B. Biddle. 1995. *The Manufactured Crisis: Myths, Fraud, and the Attack on America's Public Schools.* Reading, Mass.: Perseus.

Blau, P., and O. D. Duncan. 1967. *The American Occupational Structure.* New York: Wiley.

Bronfrenbrenner, U. 1991. What Do Families Do? *Family Affairs* 4:1–6.

Clark, R. 1983. *Family Life and School Achievement: Why Poor Black Children Succeed or Fail.* Chicago: University of Chicago Press.

Coleman, J. S., et al. 1966. *Equality of Educational Opportunity.* Washington, D.C.: U.S. Office of Education.

Comer, J. P. 1993. Inner-City Education: A Theoretical and Intervention Model. In *Sociology and the Public Agenda,* edited by W. J. Wilson. Newbury Park, Calif.: Sage.

Cummins, J. 1986. Empowering Minority Students: A Framework for Intervention. *Harvard Educational Review* 56:18–36.

Darder, A., R. D. Torres, and H. Gutierrez. 1997. *Latinos and Education: A Critical Reader.* New York: Routledge.

Edwards, C. P. 1995. Parenting Toddlers. In *Handbook of Parenting.* Vol. 1, *Children and Parenting,* edited by Marc Borstein. Mahwah, N.J.: Erlbaum.

Entwisle, D. R., and K. L. Alexander. 1996. Family Type and Children's Growth in Reading and Math over the Primary Grades. *Journal of Marriage and the Family* 58:341–45.

Entwisle, D. R., K. L. Alexander, and L. S. Olson. 1997. *Children, Schools, and Inequality.* Boulder, Colo.: Westview.

Fordham, S., and J. Ogbu. 1986. Black Students' School Success: Coping with the Burden of Acting White. *Urban Review* 18:176–201.

Frazier, E. F. 1957. *The Negro in the United States.* New York: Macmillan.

Furstenberg, F. F., Jr. 1997. The Influence of Neighborhoods on Children's Development: A Theoretical Perspective and a Research Agenda. In vol. 2 of *Neighborhood Poverty: Policy Implications in Studying Neighborhoods*, edited by J. Brooks-Gunn, G. Duncan, and J. L. Aber. New York: Russell Sage Foundation.

Furstenberg, F. F., Jr., T. D. Cook, J. Eccles, G. H. Elder, Jr., and A. Sameroff. 1999. *Managing to Make It: Urban Families and Adolescent Success.* Chicago: University of Chicago Press.

Garcia, E. E. 1997. Effective Instruction for Language Minority Students: The Teacher. In *Latinos and Education: A Critical Reader*, edited by A. Darder, R. D. Torres, and H. Gutierrez. New York: Routledge.

Glazer, N., and D. P. Moynihan. 1963. *Beyond the Melting Pot.* Cambridge: M.I.T. Press.

Grant, R. 1995. Meeting the Needs of Young Second Language Learners. In *Meeting the Challenge of Linguistic and Cultural Diversity in Early Childhood Education*, edited by E. García and B. McLaughlin, with B. Spodek and O. Saracho. New York: Teachers College Press, Columbia University.

Grossman, H. 1995. *Educating Hispanic Students: Implications for Instruction, Classroom Management, Counseling, and Assessment.* 2d ed. Springfield, Ill.: Charles Thomas.

Harrington, C. C., and S. K. Boardman. 1997. *Paths to Success: Beating the Odds in American Society.* Cambridge: Harvard University Press.

Hurst, V. 1996. Parents and Professionals: Partnership in Early Childhood Education. In *Early Childhood Education: A Developmental Curriculum*, edited by G. Blenkin and A. V. Kelly. 2d ed.. London: Paul Chapman.

Kjolseth, R. 1982. Bilingual Education Programs in the United States: For Assimilation or Pluralism? pp. 3–28 in *Bilingualism in the Southwest*, edited by P. R. Turner. 2d ed. rev. Tucson: University of Arizona Press.

Lareau, A. 1989. Family-School Relationships: A View from the Classroom. *Educational Policy* 3, no. 3:245–57.

Laosa L., and I. Sigel. 1982. *Families as Learning Environments for Children.* New York: Plenum.

Lewis, O. 1950. An Anthropological Approach To Family Studies. *American Journal of Sociology* 55, no. 5: 469–75.

——. 1959. *Five Families: Mexican Case Studies in the Culture of Poverty.* New York: Basic Books.

——. 1966. The Culture of Poverty. *Scientific American* 214, no. 10: 19–25.

Lieberman, M. 1993. *Public Education: An Autopsy.* Cambridge: Harvard University Press.

Lightfoot, S. 1978. *Worlds Apart: Relationships between Families and Schools.* NewYork: Basic Books.

Mead, L. 1986. *Beyond Entitlement: The Social Obligations of Citizenship.* New York: Free Press.

Morrison, G. S. 1991. *Early Childhood Education Today.* 5th ed. New York: Macmillan.

Peregoy, S., and O. F. Boyle. 1993. *Reading, Writing, and Learning in ESL.* New York: Academic Press.

Rado, D. 2002. School Day Falls Short in Poorer Districts. *Chicago Tribune,* September 29.

Ruiz, R. 1997. The Empowerment of Language Minority Students. In *Latinos and Education: A Critical Reader,* edited by A. Darder, R. D. Torres, and H. Gutierrez. New York: Routledge.

Sampson, W. A. 1973. The Relative Importance of Ascribed and Achieved Variables as Family Social Status Determinants. Ph.D. diss., Johns Hopkins University.

——. 2002. *Black Student Achievement: How Much Do Family and School Really Matter?* Lanham, Md.: Scarecrow.

Sánchez, G. I. 1997. History, Culture, and Education. In *Latinos and Education: A Critical Reader,* edited by A. Darder, R. D. Torres, and H. Gutierrez. New York: Routledge.

Sigel, I. 1985. A Conceptual Analysis of Beliefs. In *Parental Belief Systems,* ed. I. Sigel. Hillsdale, N.J.: Erlbaum.

Stein, N. L. 1986. *Literacy in American Schools.* Chicago: University of Chicago Press.

Steinberg, L. 1998. Standards Outside the Classroom. In *Brookings Papers on Educational Policy,* edited by D. Ravitch. Washington, D.C.: Brookings Institution.

Traub, J. 2000. Schools Are Not the Answer. *New York Times Magazine.* January, sec. 6.

Valentine, C. 1968. *Culture and Poverty.* Chicago: University of Chicago Press.

Viteritti, J. 1999. *Choosing Equality: School Choice, the Constitution, and Civil Society.* Washington, D.C.: Brookings Institute.

Winerip, M. 1998. School Choice: A New Beginning for Public Education or the Beginning of the End? *New York Times Magazine.* June, sec. 6.

ADDITIONAL SOURCES

Allen, W. B., M. B. Spencer, and G. K. Brookins, eds. 1985. *Beginnings: The Social and Affective Development of Black Children.* Hillsdale, N.J.: Erlbaum.

Anderson, E. 1990. *Streetwise: Race, Class, and Change in an Urban Community.* Chicago: University of Chicago Press.

Barber, B. K., J. E. Olson, and S. C. Shagle. 1994. Associations between Parental Psychological and Behavioral Control and Youth Internalized and Externalized Behaviors. *Child Development* 65:1120–36.

Baumrind, D. 1967. Socialization and Instrumental Competence in Young Children. In *The Young Child: Reviews of Research,* edited by W. W. Hartup. Washington, D.C.: National Association for the Education of Young Children.

———. 1971. Current Patterns of Parental Authority. *Developmental Psychology Monograph* 4, no. 1: 1–103.

Borstein, M., ed. 1995. *Handbook of Parenting.* Vol. 1, *Children and Parenting.* Mahwah, N.J.: Erlbaum.

Brooks-Gunn, J. 1995. Strategies for Altering the Outcomes of Poor Children and Their Families. In *Escape from Poverty: What Makes a Difference for Children?* edited by P. L. C. Landsdale and J. Brooks-Gunn. Cambridge: Cambridge University Press.

Bryk, D., V. E. Lee, and P. B. Holland. 1993. *Catholic Schools and the Common Good.* Cambridge: Harvard University Press.

Carnegie Corporation. 1992. *A Matter of Time.* New York: Emerson Hall.

Coleman, J. S. 1961. *The Adolescent Society.* Westport, Conn: Greenwood.

Comer, J. P. 1988. Educating Poor Minority Children. *Scientific American* 256, no. 11:42–48.

Cook, T. D., and T. R. Curtin. 1986. The Mainstream and the Underclass: Why Are the Differences So Salient and the Similarities So Unobtrusive? In *Social Comparison, Social Justice, and Relative Deprivation: Theoretical, Empirical, and Policy Perspectives,* edited by J. C. Masters and W. P. Smith. Hillsdale, N.J.: Erlbaum.

Crouter, A., S. M. MacDermid, S. M. McHale, and M. Perry-Jenkins. 1990. Parental Monitoring and Perceptions of Children's School Performance and Conduct in Dual and Single Earner Families. *Developmental Psychology* 26, no. 4:649–57.

Drake, S., and H. Cayton. 1962. *Black Metropolis: A Study of Negro Life in a Northern City.* New York: Harper & Row.

Eccles, J. S., C. Buchanan, C. F. Flanagan, A. Fuligini, C. Midgley, and D. Yee. 1991. "Control versus Autonomy during Adolescence." *Journal of Social Issues* 47, no. 4:53–68.

Epstein, J. 1987. Parental Involvement: What Research Says to Administrators. *Education and Urban Society* 19:119–36.

———. 1987. Toward a Theory of Family-School Connections: Teacher Practices and Parent Involvement. In *Social Intervention: Potential and Constraints,* edited by K. Hurrelman, F. Kaufman, and F. Lasel. Hawthorne, N.Y.: Aldine de Gruyter.

Evanston, Illinois. *Police Reported Crime.* January 1999–December 1999.

———. July 2000. *Comparison of Selected Crime and Incident Codes by Beat, Jan. 1, 1999–Dec. 31, 1999.* Supplied by the Evanston Police Department, Office of Administration, Planning Bureau.

Frazier, E. F. 1939. *The Negro Family in the United States.* Chicago: University of Chicago Press.

Friedman, M. 1962. *Capitalism and Freedom.* Chicago: University of Chicago Press.

Gans, H. J. 1995. *The War against the Poor: The Underclass and Anti-Poverty Policy.* New York: Basic Books.

Garmezy, N. 1993. Children in Poverty: Resilence despite Risk Psychiatry. *Interpersonal and Biological Processes* 56:127–36.

Giles, J. L., S. Geletta, and C. Daniels. 1994. What Makes a Good School? A Methodological Critique and Reappraisal. Paper presented at the annual meeting of The Midwest Sociological Society, March, St. Louis, Mo.

Ginsberg, H. 1986. The Myth of the Deprived Child: New Thoughts on Poor Children. In *The School Achievement of Minority children: New Perspectives,* edited by V. Neisser. Hillsdale, N.J.: Erlbaum.

Hannerz, U. 1969. *Soulside: Inquiries into Ghetto Culture and Community.* New York: Columbia University Press.

Jencks, C., and S. Mayer. 1990. The Social Consequences of Growing Up in a Poor Neighborhood. In *Inner City Poverty in the United States,* edited by L. E. Lyman and M. G. H. McGeary. Washington, D.C.: National Academy Press.

Jencks, C., and P. Peterson, eds. 1991. *The Urban Underclass.* Washington, D.C.: Brookings Institute.

Jencks, C., M. Smith, H. Ackland, M. Bane, D. Kohn, H. Gintis, B. Heyns, and S. Michelson. 1972. *Inequality: A Reassessment of the Effect of Family and Schooling in America.* New York: Basic Books.

Karweit, N. 1976. Quantity of Schooling: A Major Educational Factor? *Educational Researcher* 5, no. 2:15–17.

Katz, M. B. 1989. *The Undeserving Poor: From the War on Poverty to the War on Welfare.* New York: Pantheon.

Kelso, W. A. 1994. *Poverty and the Underclass: Changing Perceptions of the Poor in America.* New York: New York University Press.

Kotlowitz, A. 1991. *There Are No Children Here.* New York: Doubleday.

Lane, R. 1995. The Perils of School Vouchers. In *Rethinking Schools: An Agenda for Change,* edited by D. Levine, R. Lane, B. Peterson, and R. Tenoria. New York: New Press.

Lareau, A. 1989. *Home Advantage: Social Class and Parental Intervention in Elementary Education.* New York: Folmer.

Lefcourt, H. M. 1982. *Locus of Control: Current Trends in Theory and Research.* 2d ed. Hillsdale, N.J.: Erlbaum.

Lewis, H. 1967. Culture, Class, and Family Life among Low-Income Urban Negroes. In *Employment, Race, and Poverty,* edited by A. M. Ross and H. Hill. New York: Harcourt, Brace & World.

Lipset, S., and R. Bendix. 1959. *Social Mobility in Industrial Society.* Berkeley: University of California Press.

Lord, S. E., J. S. Eccles, and K. A. McCarthy. 1994. Surviving the Junior High School Transition: Family Processes and Self Perceptions As Protective and Risk Factors. *Journal of Early Adolescence* 14:162–99.

Loury, G. G. 1995. *One by One from the Inside Out: Essays and Reviews on Race and Responsibility in America.* New York: Free Press.

Mackler, B. 1971. Blacks Who Are Academically Successful. *Urban Education* 5:210–37.

Macleod, J. 1987. *Ain't No Making It: Aspirations and Attainment in a Low-Income Neighborhood.* Boulder, Colo.: Westview.

Massey, D., and N. Denton. 1993. *American Apartheid: Segregation and the Making of the Underclass.* Cambridge: Harvard University Press.

McAdoo, H. P., and J. L. McAdoo. 1985. *Black Children: Social, Educational, and Parental Environments.* Beverly Hills, Calif.: Sage.

McLanhan, S., and G. Sandefur. 1994. *Growing Up with a Single Parent: What Hurts, What Helps.* Cambridge: Harvard University Press.

Mele, A. 1995. Current Patterns of Parental Authority. *Developmental Psychology Monograph* 4, no. 1:1–103.

Murray, C. 1984. *Losing Ground: American Social Policy, 1950–80.* New York: Basic Books.

Neisser, U., ed. 1986. *The School Achievement of Minority Children.* Hillsdale, N.J.: Erlbaum.

Ogbu, J. U. 1974. *The Next Generation: An Ethnography of Education in An Urban Neighborhood.* New York: Academic Press.

———. 1986. Class, Stratification, Racial Stratification, and Schooling. In *Race, Class, and Schooling: Special Studies in Comparative Education*, no. 17, edited by L. Weis. Buffalo: SUNY Press.

———. 1990. Literacy and Schooling in Subordinate Cultures: The Case of Black Americans. In *Going to School: The African American Experience*, edited by K. Lamatey. Albany: SUNY Press.

Peterson, P. E. 1991. The Urban Underclass and the Poverty Paradox. In *The Urban Underclass*, edited by C. Jencks and P. Peterson. Washington, D.C.: Brookings Institution.

Phares, E. J. 1976. *Locus of Control in Personality.* Morristown, N.J.: General Learning Press.

Rodman, H. 1971. *Lower-Class Families: The Culture of Poverty in Negro Trinidad.* New York: Oxford University Press.

Rogoff, B., and W. Gardner. 1984. Adult Guidance of Everyday Cognition. In *Everyday Cognition: Its Development in Social Context*, edited by B. Rogoff and J. Love. Cambridge: Harvard University Press.

Rosen, B. 1959. Race, Ethnicity, and the Achievement Syndrome. *American Sociological Review* 18:176–206.

Sampson, W. A., and P. H. Rossi. 1975. Race and Family Social Standing. *American Sociological Review* 40, no. 2:201–14.

Schweinhart, L. J., H. Barnes, and D. Weikart, with W. S. Barnett and A. Epstein. 1993. *Significant Benefits: The High/Scope Perry Preschool Study through Age Twenty-seven.* Ypsilanti, Mich.: High/Scope Press.

Schweinhart, L. J., and D. Weikert. 1992. The High/Scope Perry Preschool Study, Similar Studies, and Their Implications for Public Policy in the United States. In *Early Childhood Education: Policy Issues for the 1990s*, edited by D. A. Stegelin. Norwood, N.J.: Ablex.

Scott-Jones, D. 1987. Mother as Teacher in the Families of High and Low Achieving First Graders. *Journal of Negro Education* 56, no. 1:21–34.

Stedman, L. C. 1999. An Assessment of the Contemporary Debate over U.S. Achievement. In *Brookings Papers on Educational Policy*, edited by D. Ravitch. Washington, D.C.: Brookings Institution.

Steinberg, L. S., S. Lamborn, S. Dornbusch, and N. Darling. 1992. Impact of Parenting Practices on Adolescent Achievement: Authoritative Parenting, School

Achievement, and Encouragement To Succeed. *Child Development* 63, no. 5:1266–81.

Stone, C. 1998. *Changing Urban Education.* Lawrence: University Press of Kansas.

Suskind, R. 1998. *A Hope in the Unseen: An American Odyssey from the Inner City to the Ivy League.* New York: Broadway Books.

U.S. Department of Commerce, Bureau of the Census. 1990. *1990 Census of the Population and Housing. Summary of Population and Housing Characteristics.* Illinois.

Vidich, A. J., ed. 1995. *The New Middle Classes: Life-Styles, Status Claims, and Political Orientations.* Washington Square, N.Y.: New York University Press.

Wilson, W. J. 1987. *The Truly Disadvantaged: The Inner City, the Underclass, and Public Policy.* Chicago: University of Chicago Press.

Winch, R. F. 1962. *Identification and Its Familial Determinants: Exposition of Theory and Results of Pilot Studies.* Indianapolis, Ind.: Bobbs-Merrill.

Zigler, E., and S. Styfco, eds. 1993. *Head Start and Beyond: A National Plan for Extended Childhood Intervention.* New Haven: Yale University Press.

INDEX

ABOUT THE AUTHOR

William A. Sampson has been a student of social class, race, and education for some time. It has, however, been only recently that he has begun to focus all three of these intellectual interests on the issue of the effort to educate poor, urban nonwhite students, the type of student he himself was before graduating from Howard University with a degree in sociology, the University of Wisconsin at Milwaukee with a degree in urban affairs, and Johns Hopkins University with a Ph.D. in social relations. He currently teaches at DePaul University in Chicago where the diverse student body is not only an inspiration for his work but also often an invaluable partner in that work.